C0-AKI-542

The Masterworks of Literature Series

William S. Osborne, *Editor*
Southern Connecticut State University

The Poems of Herman Melville

THE POEMS OF HERMAN MELVILLE

BY HERMAN MELVILLE

edited for the modern reader by
DOUGLAS ROBILLARD
University of New Haven

New College and University Press, Inc.
Albany, NY 12203

Copyright © 1976
College and University Press Services, Inc.
All Rights Reserved

New Material, Introduction, and Notes by
DOUGLAS ROBILLARD

Printed by:
Communication Marketing Services, Inc.
74 Yardboro Avenue, Albany NY 12205

TO
GRACE

Contents

JOHN MARR AND OTHER SAILORS

TIMOLEON, ETC.

ADDITIONAL POEMS

Introduction

Herman Melville's greatness as a writer of fiction has now been thoroughly assessed, and most of his books have been given the benefit of full explication and discussion. It is, therefore, a misfortune that a similar judgment has not been offered upon the poetry. For the most part, the anthologies of American literature have given poor representation to the poems, and relatively little commentary has been written about the poetry. The book-length studies of Melville's work concentrate upon the fiction, and useful articles dealing specifically with the poems can be quickly counted. The readily available selections of poems, those of Hennig Cohen and Robert Penn Warren, give a less rounded picture of Melville the poet than we might now wish to have, although Cohen's commentary is excellent and Warren's introduction and notes are indispensable. We owe a great debt to William Bysshe Stein and William Shurr for providing book-length commentaries on the poetry.

The purpose of this volume is to make available a substantial amount of the poetry by printing the complete contents of the three volumes of short poems that Melville saw through the press: *Battle Pieces and Aspects of the War* (1866), *John Marr and Other Sailors* (1888), and *Timoleon* (1891). We know that the author planned publication of other volumes; but he died shortly after the publication of *Timoleon*, and his remaining poems lay in manuscript until they were published in the Standard Edition (London, 1922-1924) and in the *Collected Poems*, edited by Howard P. Vincent (Chicago, 1947). I have made a selection from this group of poems and have added the version of "The Admiral of the White" that Melville published in newspapers in 1885; it does not appear in the Standard Edition

11

or in Vincent. I have not attempted to give extracts from
Clarel; this long and complex poem should be read in its
entirety.

It is to be hoped that more critical attention will now
be focused upon Melville's life and work for the period
1857-1891. His life records are few for some of these years.
We do know something about his reading, and the allu-
sions in the poetry offer a rich mine of research. Although
the Melville of these years did not produce another *Moby-
Dick*—for a variety of complex reasons, he could not—he
did write distinguished poetry; and, since he did not de-
cline into senility or indulge in aged amateurism but con-
tinued to work with a keen sense of professionalism and
a considerable expenditure of creativity, his poetic imagina-
tion is a rewarding subject for study.

II

In the poem entitled "Art," Melville gives a vivid account
of the labor of poetic creation:

> In placid hours well-pleased we dream
> Of many a brave unbodied scheme.
> But form to lend, pulsed life create,
> What unlike things must meet and mate:
> A flame to melt—a wind to freeze;
> Sad patience—joyous energies;
> Humility—yet pride and scorn;
> Instinct and study; love and hate;
> Audacity—reverence. These must mate,
> And fuse with Jacob's mystic heart,
> To wrestle with the Angel—Art.

The powerful meeting of opposites, the incalculable
strenuousness of the creative struggle, the mysterious fu-
sion, and the angelic battle—these are the elements that
come together in Melville's mind to express his feelings
about the work he so deliberately undertook, conserving
his strength and powers and using them to the best possi-
ble advantage during the last thirty years of his life.

In many ways, this phase of Melville's literary existence
is the capstone and the most disturbing aspect of an already
disturbing author. His career, from its beginnings in 1846
to its startling pause in 1856, is itself a study in contrasts

and painful contradictions. It proceeds from the young writer's keen perception of his rapidly maturing powers, his exuberant inventive faculty, and the healthy energy that he brought to his early novel writing. He must have had a rich sense of creativeness during those early years as he brought out book after book—*Typee* (1846), *Omoo* (1847), *Mardi* and *Redburn* (1849), *White Jacket* (1850), *Moby-Dick* (1851), and *Pierre* (1852). Three of the books—*Mardi, Moby-Dick*, and *Pierre*—were large-scale, demanding tasks; *Moby-Dick* might well have taken years of another artist's life to create. Further, during the composition of each of these three books, the author's mind conceived changes and additions that actually transformed the books during the act of writing them. *Mardi* changes into much more than a romantic tale of pursuit in the South Seas. *Moby-Dick* ceases to be a semi-humorous account of a whaling voyage by one Ishmael and becomes instead a grand drama of necessity, free will, chance, pride, human aspiration, and monomaniac obsession, worked into a structure that can accommodate narrative, factual information, philosophical disquisition, and poetic description. As for *Pierre*—well, if *Pierre* begins as a parody of the kind of melodramatic fiction that Melville deplored as he saw it supplanting his own work in popularity, it does not keep itself in that groove but veers off sharply toward satire, tragedy, and mythic enactment of the human drama. Read after *Moby-Dick, Pierre* is an unsettling book. It puzzles and grates; it gathers dimensions as one studies it. It is a great misfortune that the book's parts do not harmonize, though some of its parts are stunning. One of the greatest difficulties the reader must face is his knowledge that Melville was in control of all his resources as he composed the novel; he deliberately set out to do all the things he actually did. The parody of high-flown sentiment, the bathos, the banality are all devised in the most studied manner. But the trouble, as usual, with put-on sentimentality, bathos, and banality is that they are frequently about as good, or as bad, as the real thing. Melville knew this and risked it. He could be relentless in following out the logic of a conception, no matter where it led him. In *Moby-Dick*, he had adopted the attractive metaphor of the work of art as uncompleted architecture with the scaffolding still clinging to its frame. *Pierre* seems such a structure, fully finished; but the architect has left scaffolding, tools, and blocks of unused stone about, to alarm the unwary reader.

These books, requiring so much sympathetic attention, lost Melville the audience his earlier novels had brought him, and he tried, during the next few years, to capture a magazine audience. The results are as astonishing as anything he was ever to accomplish. Nothing is more excellent and artistic than *Benito Cereno* or the deeply tragicomic *Bartleby the Scrivener.* Several of the sketches making up *The Encantadas* rank with anything Melville ever wrote. Some of the shorter pieces, notably "The Bell-Tower," "Cock-a-Doodle-Doo," and "The Lightning-Rod Man," bear all the attention one may give them. By 1856, Melville had a new novel ready for publication. Read today, *The Confidence Man* seems a brilliantly successful book, absolutely certain in its technique, witty, learned, diabolically clever in its fluid metamorphoses of themes and characters. Its satirical treatment of the Transcendentalists is funny, pointed, and thoroughly beguiling. Its prevailing tone is acrid and pungent, but it can plunge into seriousness when the occasion is available. There is not a more poised book in all of Melville's work; it should be read as a central document in the development of the author's art, only less important than *Moby-Dick* or the great novellas.

Melville's life from the completion of *The Confidence Man* in 1856 to his confirmation, more or less, in the profession of poetry by 1860, needs close scrutiny. We know something of his feelings as he completed the novel and prepared to go to Europe and the Near East. On September 1, 1856, Lemuel Shaw wrote of Melville's apparent illness and speculated that his concentration upon his literary work was the cause. Medical opinion apparently declared that his health was seriously undermined and that he must give up the strenuous work of novel writing. In the middle of October he sailed and, during the journey, kept a journal as tantalizing for what it does not say as for what it manages to record. His visit with Hawthorne is a case in point. Melville's journal entry is a bare "saw Mr. Hawthorne"; but Hawthorne's account is much more revealing.

The journal entries in his *English Notebooks* speak of Melville's neuralgic complaints, the too great intensity of his literary labors, and his morbid state of mind. He records some of their conversation, including Melville's statement that he had "pretty well made up his mind to be annihilated." Hawthorne's continuation is of the greatest interest: "He can neither believe, nor be comfortable in his unbelief; and he is too honest and courageous not to try to do one or the other." A religious crisis, then, with a powerful drive to resolve it; morbidity; an illness seemingly brought on by literary exertions that were not being appropriately recognized; a warning from doctors that he must give up such labors for the sake of his health—all worked together to lead Melville in the direction his future work was to take. Add to this the feeling that he had lost the audiences he had tried to win for his fiction and that few seemed to comprehend what he was doing; add the failure of his attempts as a lecturer from 1857 to 1860; add, too, his persistent idea that a move to New York might gain him a job in the custom house, a job he appears to have made every effort to secure; and we begin to sense some of the complex reasons behind his change of profession.

It is not that poetry, in any case, represented a radical departure for Melville. The author who stubbornly began a career as a poet some time after 1857 was, in fact, already a poet. He had written more than twenty poems for *Mardi*, and some of these already had shown his talent. For *Moby-Dick*, he had introduced a hymn as part of Father Mapple's service, and, although this was an adaptation of an existing hymn, Melville's changes and excisions display a masterly sense of poetic form. It may even be that his work as a poet went back to the very beginnings of his career as a writer. In 1845, the publishing firm of William M. Christy issued in New York an anonymous book-length poem entitled *Redburn: or the Schoolmaster at Morning*, a limp little narrative in four cantos. The possibilities are far from conclusive, depending only upon the title of Melville's own novel; and it is better to dwell upon what we do know of our poet.

We got glimpses of Melville during the last months of his efforts as a lecturer and the start of his full-time poetic career. A visitor in April of 1859 characterized him as a disappointed man, "soured by criticism and disgusted with the civilized world and with our Christendom in general and in particular"; another found that he had shut himself up "as a cloistered thinker." He was writing poetry and, by 1860, had enough to submit a volume to Scribners; the publisher rejected the book.

It would be of great interest to know what was in that abortive volume of poems; probably, some of the poems left in manuscript at Melville's death made up part of the book. In the first years of the 1860's were beginning to occur the great events that Melville would record in *Battle Pieces*. He took a keen interest in the Civil War, following the printed accounts, the *Rebellion Record*, the newspapers, and the magazines he had been accustomed to read. He almost certainly read Hawthorne's anonymous article, "Chiefly About War Matters," when it appeared in the *Atlantic Monthly* in July, 1862.[1] The *Atlantic* was full of material well fitted in catch his eye and offer materials for his poems. There were articles on soldier poems and on the battle of Antietam; the magazine printed Longfellow's poem about the warship *Cumberland*, a subject Melville would want to treat.

We should probably accept Melville's word in the note to *Battle Pieces* that his writing of most of the poems came after the fall of Richmond in April, 1865. It is possible that what he had written before this time was of a miscellaneous nature, on subjects that had stirred him as he heard about them. As the poems accumulated, they must have come to assume a shape and coherence as a group; and, stimulated by this sense of order, he sought to stitch the book together, writing more poems to fill in the gaps. A characteristic of Melville's poetic nature is that he is seldom content to publish a miscellaneous collection of poems but must attempt to impose an order upon each volume. Early in 1866, he began to publish some of the war poems in *Harper's New Monthly Magazine*, and in August Harper issued the book, a fairsized collection of seventy-two poems with a preface and a prose supplement. It may be easy to underrate the extent of Melville's achievement in this volume; a number of critics

---

1. See Leo B. Levy, "Hawthorne, Melville, and the Monitor," *American Literature*, XXXVII (1965), 33-40.

have managed to do just that. On the other hand, Robert Penn Warren, Richard Fogle, and Hennig Cohen offer impressive evidence of its quality. Like Whitman's *Drum Taps*, it is a war book that should be read through rather than in selection, for the whole makes a stronger impression than the parts.

The pattern of the book is chronological. It proceeds through poems of foreboding and misgivings, to descriptions of battles, to comments upon the horrors of war, to moments of pride and moments of depression, to the conclusion of the war, the death of Lincoln, memorials for the war dead, the final dignified stance of Lee, and, at the end, Melville's own statement of summary and hope. One may well find that, at times, the book is unified more by determination than by art and that the plan is often filled by the insertion of weak and mediocre poems. But few can deny that its best poems are superb. The reader should be aware of the quality of "Misgivings," "Shiloh," "The March into Virginia," "The College Colonel," "Formerly a Slave," and "The Apparition." Melville's night-piece, "The House-Top," is as notable for its poetical nature as for its political coloring:

> No sleep. The sultriness pervades the air
> And binds the brain—a dense oppression, such
> As tawny tigers feel in matted shades,
> Vexing their blood and making apt for ravage.
> Beneath the stars the roofy desert spreads
> Vacant as Libya.

The finest poem in the volume is the first one, "The Portent," and it sets the tone of the entire work. Here, in two stanzas, Melville captures a rhythm of ominous expectation and gravity. His poetic technique is mature and his point is made with an economy of words and vivid imagery:

> Hidden in the cap
>   Is the anguish none can draw;
> So your future veils its face,
>   Shenandoah!
> But the streaming beard is shown
>   (Weird John Brown),
> The meteor of the war.

These are poems at the top of Melville's bent; but he speaks in a variety of poetic voices, and the book contains much that should be examined. The naval poems were likely to bring out the best in his love for the sea, and they do make a worthy group. They include "Dupont's Round Fight," "The Temeraire," "The Stone Fleet," "The Cumberland," "In the Turret," and "A Utiliteration View of the Monitor's Fight"; in them we see an affection for the past of the old wooden ships, an elegiac feeling at the passing of that time; and an ironic bafflement at the new world of submarines, ironclads, and war made a business of detachment or passionless calculation.

Many of the poems are narratives which betray erratically Melville's already proven skill as a storyteller. "Donelson" seems an unsuccessful piece, but it should interest the student of Melville's narrative art to see how the poet goes about solving a number of his problems by bringing in a number of varied technical effects; he uses a letter, newspaper headlines, conversation, and he gives reports timed to the hour to maintain tension and to diversify the texture of the poem. An even longer narrative, "The Scout Toward Aldie," is a thoroughly attractive account of a raid by Union cavalry attempting to engage the heroic and nearly mythic Mosby. The story is skillfully told, transitions are sharply marked to keep the narrative moving, and Melville's use of poetic language is remarkably fresh. But, because of the skills lavished upon it, the poem is almost heartbreaking. If Melville could handle the theme of war so well in his poetry, what a great Civil War novel he could have given us! It was left to John W. DeForest to do what Melville might have done in the quarter century after the war. The loss is incalculable.

We must measure the seriousness of Melville's intentions by the prose supplement that he used to end *Battle Pieces*. It is a careful and reasonable argument for just, charitable disposition of the defeated South. "Let us be Christians to our fellow-whites, as well as philanthropists toward the blacks, our fellow-men," he says. His concern for his country overrides artistic considerations. Knowing that the supplement can only harm the artistic integrity of the whole volume, he still feels that he must include it. His concern is justifiable and produces a document that should be read, and probably is not, by every historian of the war. The last brief paragraph is especially pertinent and moving:

> Let us pray that the great historic tragedy of our time may not have been enacted without instructing our whole beloved country through terror and pity; and may fulfillment verify in the end those expectations which kindle the bards of Progress and Humanity.

III

In October of 1863, Melville and his family moved from Pittsfield to New York City and began a long residence at 104 East 26th Street. A visit to the battlefront occupied him in the spring of the next year, and the composition of the poems for *Battle Pieces* was the work of 1865 and 1866. In December, 1866, he finally received the appointment he had long wanted as an inspector of Customs, and this appointment was to regularize his life and send it into an unaccustomed groove for the next twenty years. The family was happy about the job; his mother noted that his being compelled to go to business had improved his health. What Melville thought of the changed condition of his existence is not recorded, but the evidence is that it did help his health, provide earnings for his family, let him keep his troubled spirit in check, and very likely helped to ease his depression and especially the strain caused by the suicide of his son Malcolm in September of 1867.

All that was to happen to Melville for the remainder of his life happened quietly. He worked in the Custom House till December, 1885, when he could retire at age 65. During quite a number of these years, he was busily engaged in writing *Clarel*, a lengthy poem that he finally published in 1876. His wife considered it a "dreadful incubus of a book" and was relieved when it was finally completed. In 1875 she had written "Herman is pretty well and very busy—pray do not mention to *any one* that he is writing poetry—you know how such things spread and he would be very angry if he knew I had spoken of it." So his composition of the poem was a kind of tacit, unmentionable subject that must have affected his own feelings as he went on relentlessly with the huge task he had set himself.

There is, indeed, something relentless, excessively stubborn, in Melville's nature as he addresses himself to a job. It had carried him through the brilliantly managed composition of *Moby-Dick* in an astonishingly short time. It had certainly persisted in his work on *Pierre*, a far less inspired novel. It had surely led to the physical, spiritual, and mental pressures that had caused his illness and forced him to turn away from the writing of fiction. It is to be found in his unremitting labors upon *Clarel*. One hardly knows what to do about *Clarel*. If one is fanatical enough about Melville so that nothing less than the whole man and the whole work will be enough, he is likely to study the poem enthusiastically. He may even lose perspective and come at last to believe that it is the center of Melville, known only to the fortunate few. On the other hand, if the best of Melville is enough for the reader, he will not feel obliged to read *Clarel* at all.

Reading it is a back-breaking task. In the most personal terms, it is doubtless a book that Melville simply had to write. It seems unlikely that he could have gone on as he did if he had not pushed this Sisyphean stone as far as his shoulders could take it. Annihilation—physical annihilation—might well have been the consequence of not writing it. And so, without being more than sporadically interesting and successful, the poem is a deeply significant document in the long travail of Melville's later life. It is a key to his further development as a writer, and it must have been a catharsis for his troubled spirit. For in it he wrestled with his unbelief and his hope for a belief, and he could not rest till he had somehow, to his own satisfaction, at any rate, handled fully the conflicts in his own nature. One turns away from *Clarel* with a sigh of compassion for so much waste.

After *Clarel*, one's attention is occupied by Melville's reading, his work on his poetry and upon *Billy Budd*. We need a fuller account of these quiet years, for they produced some of Melville's best poetic work. Of his published volumes of poetry, *John Marr and Other Sailors* has the strongest claim to represent the poetic best that was in Melville. Individual poems in the volume are composed with high art, but it is profitable to see the book as a coherent whole. The evidence that Melville intended it to be read as a whole is unmistakable. The issues the book raises must have been dear to him; they must have been meaningful in an extremely personal way. He presents a sailor who is also a poet; this is the story of a man who has been cut off from the sea, that stringent and deadly but life-giving and healing force. He has been alienated among landlubbers who can no more understand his visions than he can share theirs; and he must turn to memory and poetry to heal his wounds. What autobiographical meaning there is in this book, what a response, for Melville, to the incomprehension of the world that first listened and then rejected his artistic offerings! His public had been like the farmer who heard John Marr spin his tales of the sea and then commented, "Friend we know nothing of that here." One imagines how the book could give the author a profound sense of satisfaction to realize how secure his poetic control was here and how deeply he was moving into his own psyche.

The plan of the book is quite clear. In the prose scenario that opens the story, Melville lays before us the situation of his hurt poet—Marr is condition as well as name—who has lost the sea, his companions, his past, his wife and child, and any sense of social, cultural, or spiritual integration into his inland community. He has gone into the physical heartland and found emptiness, for, "with nobody to blame, he is obstructed"; he must dive now into his spiritual heartland to recover his existence. He must conjure up his friends, the other sailors, the world that is vivid in his memory, and must bring them into living poetry.

As John Marr's thoughts turn back to the sea, it becomes the central theme and symbol of the book, portrayed poetically in all its aspects.[2] It is, first of all, a cruel sea, destructive of men and ships. In "The Aeolian Harp," the central image is that of a wrecked vessel, "Bulwarks gone—a shaven

2. Here I have adapted material from my article, "Theme and Structure in Melville's *John Marr and Other Sailors*," *English Language Notes*, VI (March, 1969), 187-192. Thanks are due to the editors of ELN for allowing me to make use of the article.

wreck,/Nameless, and a grass-green deck." The poem then goes on to mourn the sailors shipwrecked and lost. Other poems continue the theme of the sea's destructiveness: in "Far Off-Shore," a raft is discovered, empty of life; in "The Berg," a ship collides with an iceberg, a massive engine of fate, and sinks. In "The Haglets," one of Melville's most successful poems, fate and the sea conspire to destroy a victorious warship and its crew. The final set of poems in the volume, seven brief and rather cryptic epigrams collectively entitled "Pebbles," sums up and generalizes the experience of the sea's cruelty. In these poems, the sea is described as unpredictable, alien to man, implacable, and inhuman. The fourth poem of the series, a single couplet, ironically epitomizes the relationship of sea and man: "On ocean where the embattled fleets repair,/Man, suffering inflictor, sails on sufferance there."

However, cruel as it can be, the sea is also a medium of health, a cleaner, sharper element than we usually dwell in. A brief quatrain, "The Tuft of Kelp," must be read in this light:

> All dripping in tangles green,
> Cast up by a lonely sea
> If purer for that, O Weed,
> Bitterer, too, are ye?

In its brief span, the poem catches up both sides of Melville's complex feeling about the sea: a bitter and lonely habitation for man, it can purify him as well. The paradox is restated brilliantly in the final poem of "Pebbles," which is also the last poem in the volume and thus bears the heaviest burden of the sailor-poet's meditation upon his chosen theme. Sick and alienated by things of the land, John Marr is made well again by his vision of the sea:

> Healed of my hurt, I laud the inhuman Sea—
> Yea, bless the Angels Four that there convene;
> For healed I am even by their pitiless breath
> Distilled in wholesome dew named rosmarine.

Rosmarine is rosemary, and it is surely for remembrance; but it is also *ros marinus*, the "sea-dew," a plant that grows at the sea's edge. The inhumanity of the sea is inseparable from its healing powers.

As a result of these beliefs about the sea, the attitudes of those who dwell at sea are often contrasted with those of land-dwellers. Living far from his beloved sea, in the middle of the midwestern prairies, John Marr sees the rolling land as a kind of ocean floor, unmarked and uninhabited, empty of the stir of life that characterizes the sea. The course that Nature takes in the two environments is sharply contrasted as well. Death and destruction can come swiftly and violently at sea, as in "The Berg" and "The Haglets." The Maldive shark, "pale ravener of horrible meat," is the typical denizen of this unfriendly element. But, in spite of its alien character and its capacity for horror, the sea is an arena in which man can act. He takes things "as fated merely," holds life less than dear, and finds his meanings in the responses he makes to the harsh life about him. In the first poem, John Marr enunciates the motto, *"Life is storm—let storm."* On land, however, far from being in such a dynamic bond with Nature, man is unobtrusively bested by it. The farm people who are the sailor's neighbors are "staid through habituation to monotonous hardship; ascetic by necessity." Their lack of response to his accounts of his adventures at sea seems "of a piece with the apathy of Nature herself." There are no horrors, no violent deaths upon the land, but one cannot imagine it capable of healing powers. The asceticism of landlocked existence is directly counter to the richness of John Marr's oceanic imagination.

The unity provided by the interrelation of themes is supported by a structural unity, for Melville has fitted the poems into a dramatic context which is preserved without lapse throughout the volume. The prose scenario with which Melville opens the work recounts the story of the sailor's retirement from the sea, his employment in various occupations, his marriage, the deaths of his wife and child, and his settlement at the place where they are buried, far inland. Here, because of his isolation from the sea and his alienation from the landsmen, because of his lack of a responsive relationship with Nature, he must turn inward and let his mind dwell lyrically upon the past, his former friends, and his life at sea. In this introductory portion, Melville seems to be limiting the point of view of the whole volume to John Marr, but, just as he does not scruple to move from the point of view of Ishmael in *Moby-Dick*, here he does not restrict himself. The concluding couplet of the first poem, "To see you at the halyards main—/To hear your chorus once again" makes way for the narratives of the "other sailors" of the title and gives them freedom to speak in their own voices. In the two poems that follow, "Bridegroom Dick" and "Tom Deadlight," we then have two of the sailors offering their monologues. Since John Marr is imagined as speaking from retirement not long before the Civil War —the date of Tom Deadlight's dying soliloquy is given as 1810, and the date from which Dick looks back upon the past is 1876—Melville's historical view is broadened enormously beyond the confines of one sailor's reminiscence. The poems thus exhibit in dramatic manner one of the themes, the effect of change over a long period of time and the opposition of the sailor temperament to such change. In such a way, the inserted prose and the varied points of view used in the dramatic monologues help to provide a structure for the varied elements of the volume.

As a further structural device to hold the book together, Melville provides a kind of plot for the reader to follow through the successive poems as his protagonist passes from the condition of depression and illness to recovery and health. In the prose scenario which prefaces the poems, John Marr is portrayed in a state of mental distress. Although he has ceased somewhat to mourn his family, "the void at heart abides." Since it is a void caused by more than personal grief, nothing comes to fill it until his consciousness begins to turn creatively to a consideration of the poetry of his past, his friends, the sea, and the human condition. Then his return to health is dramatically presented. He takes part in the lives of other sailors, even those of other times, and is a witness to their deaths; he is reminded of the terrors of the sea and of its stringent curative and purifying powers. He remembers the master of the vessel, *Meteor*, and drinks a toast to him. Significantly for Melville's biography, the poem is revised from the earlier "To Tom," and addressed to Melville's brother, Thomas Melville (1830-1883), who had a career at sea and was master of the *Meteor*. Healed finally of his hurt, the poet is like the tuft of kelp which came up from the sea purer and bitterer; he comes up from the immersion in his vision feeling more realistic, bit-

terer, purer from the cathartic value of experiencing once
again the sea in all its sympathy and terror.

After the publication of *John Marr* Melville had three
more years, and we may judge that they were busy, produc-
tive years. He crowned his great efforts in fiction by pro-
ducing the magnificent *Billy Budd*, a tale that grows, ap-
propriately enough, out of a poem, "Billy in the Darbies,"
and the prose headnote he had planned to attach to it. One
of the most interesting aspects of his poetic development
is this continual movement from poetry to prose and back
again. As we have seen, he wanted a prose supplement to
complete *Battle Pieces*, though he did not attempt to stitch
it into the fabric of the book and was uneasy about its artistic
propriety. The prose in *John Marr* is perfectly suited to the
matter of the poetry; the opening prose piece sets up the con-
ditions under which the poems are allowed to exist, and the
prose headnote of "Tom Deadlight" establishes the back-
ground of the poem. Again and again he was to bring poetry
and prose together, trying to fuse them into an artistic whole.
In *Billy Budd*, the prose flowers luxuriantly into a short
novel and the poem is tacked on at the end, perfectly satis-
factory as a poem but less than compelling as a conclusion
to the tale.

The tale itself is brilliant and exemplary, a dramatic
working out of the principles of fate, chance, and free will
that Melville had let Ishmael expound in the forty-seventh
chapter of *Moby-Dick*. So deeply significant is the careful
setting out of all the elements necessary for this inevit-
able tragedy, that the characters, as vividly imagined as they
are, must yield to the sweep of the narrative. Melville sets
forth the only possible chain of conditions and events that
could lead to such a conclusion. The background of the
Nore and *Spithead* rebellions and the makeup of the ships'
crews help to shape the attitudes of the officers toward their
men. The sailor impressed by the British cannot be other
than Billy, handsome and an object of desire, powerful
enough to strike a fatal blow, blocked from free discourse
or facile explanation by his stammer. Claggart, nearly inex-
plicable except as an example of absolute depravity, and in-
timately involved in a relationship of love and hate with
Billy, is an inevitable catalyst to tragedy. Most of all, Cap-

tain Vere is needed, as captain and god and man. The flaw in his nature seems a small thing: when he is on deck in a dreamy and introspective mood and is interrupted, he becomes wrathful and somewhat irrational. But the flaw gives impetus to the tragedy. What other ship's captain, irate at being interrupted by Claggart's stupid and spiteful story, would allow accuser and accused to face each other, without restraints of any kind, in his cabin? How much saner to arrest Budd, put him in irons, and investigate the story? The workings of transcendent powers, as the author views them, would not allow such a solution.

We must assume that Melville selected and placed the poems he assembled for his last published collection, *Timoleon*, as carefully as he had done for *John Marr*. He assumed responsibility for the printing and binding of both volumes in inexpensive paperback form in editions of twenty-five copies. He probably felt he could afford no more for grander ventures. One senses in this the powerful urge toward publication, mixed, no doubt, with the desire not to be turned down once more by publishers and public. With his keen perceptions about the relationship of the artist to his work and his public, he must have appreciated the irony of these little efforts, handled much as an amateur, eager to be printed for the first time, might have handled them. His sense of the situation seems well reflected in his poem, "The Ravaged Villa":

> In shards the sylvan vases lie,
>   Their links of dance undone,
> And brambles wither by thy brim,
>   Choked fountains of the sun!
> The spider in the laurel spins,
>   The weed exiles the flower:
> And, flung to kiln, Apollo's bust
>   Makes lime for Mammon's tower.

It is no accident that *Timoleon* and the uncollected manuscript poems return again and again to the artist's predicament. In the published volume we have "Art," "The Weaver," "In a Garret," "Shelley's Vision," "Pisa's Leaning Tower," "Milan Cathedral," "The Parthenon," "The Attic Landscape," "Greek Architecture," and "Disinterment of the Hermes" all displaying Melville's vision of art, his painful and rewarding preoccupation with the exacting conditions of the life he had lived for more than forty years. The poems are touching, even the smallest scaled and most reserved of them. Following Melville's career through so many turns and brilliances, so many alienations and returns, one is moved by the presence behind these late statements. The preoccupation with art continues in the uncollected poems. "Immolation" is addressed directly to poems that have been destroyed, and "Camoens," "Montaigne and his Kitten," "The Rusty Man," and "The Medallion" continue the poet's meditation upon his art.

Other poems in *Timoleon* reflect the range of Melville's reading and interests. The title poem is based upon the story Plutarch tells in his life of Timoleon, but it may also have been influenced by a reading of Balzac. A more interesting poem is "After the Pleasure Party." Its subject is just what its epigraph points out—Amor threatening the urge to decline love in favor of other pursuits—and it delineates vividly the ill effects of rejecting the sexual side of our nature. The poet moves easily from dramatic monologue to narrative, from musing to passionate outburst to argument:

> Could I remake me! or set free
> This sexless bound in sex, then plunge
> Deeper than Sappho in a lunge
> Piercing Pan's paramount mystery!
> For, Nature, in no shallow surge
> Against thee either sex may urge,
> Why hast thou made us but in halves—
> Co-relatives? This makes us slaves
> If these co-relatives never meet
> Self-hood itself seems incomplete.
> And such the dicing of blind fate
> Few matching halves here meet and mate.
> What Cosmic jest or Anarch blunder
> The human integral clove asunder
> And shied the fractions through life's gate?

The language is bold, its sexuality unmistakable. It is perhaps this strength that might in part account for Melville's desire to publish in small editions, privately, and anonymously. During the generation when he was writing, Whitman had spoken out boldly on sexual matters in his poems and had suffered the consequences. James and Twain, among others, were hampered by the common agreement that such matters were not to be dealt with in literature. As a powerful figure in the editorial circles of Boston and New York, Howells complacently told readers what things should not be put in books and then showed the way by leaving them out of his extraordinarily well-written novels. But Melville wanted to get the sexual matter into his writing. In the *John Marr* volume, the long poem, "Bridegroom Dick," is full of sly sexual allusions and has a lusty, vulgar humor to it that is hearty and enlivening. The uncollected poems turn the subject around for examination, and, in "Pontoosuc," the poet has life and death mingle in an erotic embrace.

Beyond this, there is considerable variety and excellence to be found in *Timoleon*. Consider the brief poem entitled "Buddha":

> Swooning swim to less and less,
>   Aspirant to nothingness!
> Sobs of the worlds, and dole of kinds
>   That dumb endurers be—
> Nirvana! absorb us in your skies
>   Annul us into thee.

Melville thickens the texture of the poem by adding from the Bible an epigraph not much shorter than the poem itself: "For what is your life? It is even a vapor, that appeareth for a little time, and then vanisheth away" (James iv :14). Melville is back with the Transcendentalists, and Emerson is still Mark Winsome. The "Monody," a touching elegy, is generally taken to be Melville's response, however long after the event, to Hawthorne's death. It may be so; he composed the poem on a flyleaf of one of Hawthorne's books. But the estrangement in the poem hardly seems to suggest the relationship between the two writers; and the poem might just as well be about Malcolm, the son who committed suicide in 1867.

All in all, *Timoleon*, quite different from *John Marr* in its scope and themes, not by any means bound into a coherent unit as the earlier book is, offers a firmly composed collection that displays the modulations of Melville's poetic talent. Unfortunately, it was to be the last book that Melville would see through the press. It was printed in June, 1891, and on September 28 its author died. He had attempted, at various times, to ready other volumes of poetry for publication. A combination of poetry and prose was assembled under the title of *Weeds and Wildings*, and the format in which it comes to us offers some opportunity for study. It is a mixed performance; some of the poems sound like the sort of thing that Melville would have us believe the young Pierre had written before his unfortunate flight from Saddle Meadows. One of the most interesting pieces in the proposed volume is "Rip Van Winkle's Lilac," in part because Melville comes back once more to the fusion of prose and poetry in a single work. The device works well in *John Marr* and the working from poetry to prose in *Billy Budd* is a triumphant solution to a specific problem. "Rip Van Winkle's Lilac" is a thoroughly readable piece of prose that turns into a not very interesting poem. The piece should be examined as a set of variations upon Irving's tale, a colloquy with Death upon the subject of Art, and a statement of the triumph of life forces—Rip, the lilac bush, art—over death.

Of all the poems left in manuscript, by far the best is "Pontoosuc."[3] The manuscript shows considerable labor of revision. The poem is remarkable, rich in language and imagery, evoking the spirit of death and deeply pondering the lesson of mortality in all things. The spirit who appears to the poet reconciles the opposing arguments with her recitation of the cycle of living and dying, waxing and wan-

---

3. There is some controversy about the title. The Standard Edition prints the poem with the discarded title, "The Lake." O. F. Matthiessen's little pamphlet selection of Melville's poems (New Directions, 1946) gives the title "The Lake," with "Pontoosuc" as subtitle. Vincent's *Collected Poems* makes the title out to be "Pontoosuce," and Robert Penn Warren insists rather strongly upon this spelling. I am all for "Pontoosuc"; that is the name of the lake near his home in Pittsfield, and it is difficult to tell whether the manuscript is blessed with a final letter or a careless doodle.

ing, ending and beginning. The conclusion is a vividly dramatic act:

> She kissed me, while her chaplet cold
> Its rootlets brushed against my brow,
> With all their humid clinging mould.
> She vanished, leaving fragrant breath
> And warmth and chill of wedded life and death.

Life and the grave, warmth and cold, mould and rootlets—all mingle easily in the poem as in the natural order of the universe.

Only a study of the poems can give us a sufficiently clear picture of Melville as an artist. It is important to remember that the creative imagination that burned so brightly in his youth did not sputter and die out after *The Confidence Man*. The spirit continued its search in spite of painful times and distracted wandering after sterile goals; nor did the catastrophes of his life cause Melville to do what some have imagined—to lapse into cranky old age and amateurism till he was revived for once by the challenge of *Billy Budd*. This did not happen. For more than thirty years, after giving up the writing of prose fiction, Melville practiced seriously the arduous craft of his poetry. The miracle is that the poet in him survived, gathered strength, and made his later art a distinctive element in his creative existence.

Acknowledgments

I owe a debt of thanks to the Houghton Library at Harvard for allowing me to study the manuscripts of Melville's poems and for giving me permission to print several that did not appear during Melville's lifetime; to the Beinecke Library at Yale for allowing me to use its nineteenth-century editions of the poems; and to Nat Kaplan, whose death robbed us of a stern and friendly critic.

Douglas Robillard

New Haven, Connecticut
July, 1976

BATTLE PIECES
AND ASPECTS OF THE WAR

[WITH few exceptions, the Pieces in this volume origi-
nated in an impulse imparted by the fall of Richmond.
They were composed without reference to collective
arrangement, but, being brought together in review,
naturally fall into the order assumed.

The events and incidents of the conflict—making up
a whole, in varied amplitude, corresponding with the
geographical area covered by the war—from these but a
few themes have been taken, such as for any cause chanced
to imprint themselves upon the mind.

The aspects which the strife as a memory assumes are
as manifold as are the moods of involuntary medita-
tion—moods variable, and at times widely at variance.
Yielding instinctively, one after another, to feelings not
inspired from any one source exclusively, and unmindful,
without purposing to be, of consistency, I seem, in most
of these verses, to have but placed a harp in a window,
and noted the contrasted airs which wayward winds have
played upon the strings.]

THE PORTENT
(1859)

Hanging from the beam,
  Slowly swaying (such the law),
Gaunt the shadow on your green,
  Shenandoah!
The cut is on the crown
(Lo, John Brown),
And the stabs shall heal no more.

Hidden in the cap
  Is the anguish none can draw;
So your future veils its face,
  Shenandoah!
But the streaming beard is shown
(Weird John Brown),
The meteor of the war.

MISGIVINGS
(1860)

When ocean-clouds over inland hills
  Sweep storming in late autumn brown,
And horror the sodden valley fills,
  And the spire falls crashing in the town,
I muse upon my country's ills—
The tempest bursting from the waste of Time
On the world's fairest hope linked with man's foulest crime.

Nature's dark side is heeded now—
  (Ah! optimist-cheer disheartened flown)—
A child may read the moody brow
  Of yon black mountain lone.
With shouts the torrents down the gorges go,
  And storms are formed behind the storm we feel:
The hemlock shakes in the rafter, the oak in the driving keel.

THE CONFLICT OF CONVICTIONS[a]
(1860-1)

On starry heights
  A bugle wails the long recall;
Derision stirs the deep abyss,
  Heaven's ominous silence over all.
Return, return, O eager Hope,
  And face man's latter fall.
Events, they make the dreamers quail;
Satan's old age is strong and hale,
A disciplined captain, gray in skill,
And Raphael a white enthusiast still;
Dashed aims, at which Christ's martyrs pale,
Shall Mammon's slaves fulfill?

  (Dismantle the fort,
  Cut down the fleet—
  Battle no more shall be!
  While the fields for fight in æons to come
  Congeal beneath the sea.)

The terrors of truth and dart of death
  To faith alike are vain;
Though comets, gone a thousand years,
  Return again,
Patient she stands—she can no more—
And waits, nor heeds she waxes hoar.

  (At a stony gate,
  A statue of stone,
  Weed overgrown—
  Long 'twill wait!)

But God his former mind retains,
  Confirms his old decree;
The generations are inured to pains,
  And strong Necessity
Surges, and heaps Time's strand with wrecks.
  The People spread like a weedy grass,
  The thing they will bring to pass,
And prosper to the apoplex.

The rout it herds around the heart,
    The ghost is yielded in the gloom;
Kings wag their heads—Now save thyself
    Who wouldst rebuild the world in bloom.

> *(Tide-mark*
> *And top of the ages' strife,*
> *Verge where they called the world to come,*
> *The last advance of life—*
> *Ha ha, the rust on the Iron Dome!)*

Nay, but revere the hid event;
    In the cloud a sword is girded on,
I mark a twinkling in the tent
    Of Michael the warrior one.
Senior wisdom suits not now,
The light is on the youthful brow.

> *(Ay, in caves the miner see:*
> *His forehead bears a taper dim;*
> *Darkness so he feebly braves—*
> *A meagre wight!)*

But He who rules is old—is old;
Ah! faith is warm, but heaven with age is cold.

> *(Ho ho, ho ho,*
> *The cloistered doubt*
> *Of olden times*
> *Is blurted out!)*

The Ancient of Days forever is young,
    Forever the scheme of Nature thrives;
I know a wind in purpose strong—
    It spins *against* the way it drives.
What if the gulfs their slimed foundations bare?
So deep must the stones be hurled
Whereon the throes of ages rear
The final empire and the happier world.

> *(The poor old Past,*
> *The Future's slave,*
> *She drudged through pain and crime*
> *To bring about the blissful Prime,*
> *Then—perished. There's a grave!)*

Power unanointed may come—
Dominion (unsought by the free)
  And the Iron Dome,
Stronger for stress and strain,
Fling her huge shadow athwart the main;
But the Founders' dream shall flee.
Age after age shall be
As age after age has been,
(From man's changeless heart their way they win);
And death be busy with all who strive—
Death, with silent negative.

YEA AND NAY—
EACH HATH HIS SAY;
BUT GOD HE KEEPS THE MIDDLE WAY.
NONE WAS BY
WHEN HE SPREAD THE SKY;
WISDOM IS VAIN, AND PROPHESY.

APATHY AND ENTHUSIASM
(1860-1)

I

O the clammy cold November,
  And the winter white and dead,
And the terror dumb with stupor,
  And the sky a sheet of lead;
And events that came resounding
  With the cry that *All was lost*,
Like the thunder-cracks of massy ice
  In intensity of frost—
Bursting one upon another
  Through the horror of the calm.
  The paralysis of arm
In the anguish of the heart;
And the hollowness and dearth.
  The appealings of the mother
  To brother and to brother
Not in hatred so to part—

And the fissure in the hearth
    Growing momently more wide.
Then the glances 'tween the Fates,
    And the doubt on every side,
And the patience under gloom
In the stoniness that waits
The finality of doom.

II

So the winter died despairing,
    And the weary weeks of Lent;
And the ice-bound rivers melted,
    And the tomb of Faith was rent.
O, the rising of the People
    Came with springing of the grass,
They rebounded from dejection
    After Easter came to pass.
And the young were all elation
    Hearing Sumter's cannon roar.
And they thought how tame the Nation
    In the age that went before.
And Michael seemed gigantical,
    The Arch-fiend but a dwarf;
And at the towers of Erebus
    Our striplings flung the scoff.
But the elders with foreboding
    Mourned the days forever o'er,
And recalled the forest proverb,
    The Iroquois' old saw;
Grief to every graybeard
    When young Indians lead the war.

THE MARCH INTO VIRGINIA
ENDING IN THE FIRST MANASSAS
(July, 1861)

Did all the lets and bars appear
  To every just or larger end,
Whence should come the trust and cheer?
  Youth must its ignorant impulse lend—
Age finds place in the rear.
  All wars are boyish, and are fought by boys,
The champions and enthusiasts of the state:
   Turbid ardors and vain joys
    Not barrenly abate—
Stimulants to the power mature,
   Preparatives of fate.

Who here forecasteth the event?
What heart but spurns at precedent
And warnings of the wise,
Contemned foreclosures of surprise?
The banners play, the bugles call,
The air is blue and prodigal.
  No berrying party, pleasure-wooed,
No picnic party in the May,
Ever went less loth than they
  Into that leafy neighborhood.
In Bacchic glee they file toward Fate,
Moloch's uninitiate;
Expectancy, and glad surmise
Of battle's unknown mysteries.
All they feel is this: 'tis glory,
A rapture sharp, though transitory,
Yet lasting in belaureled story.
So they gayly go to fight.
Chatting left and laughing right.

But some who this blithe mood present,
  As on in lightsome files they fare,
Shall die experienced ere three days be spent—
  Perish, enlightened by the vollied glare;
Or shame survive, and, like to adamant,
  The throe of Second Manassas share.

LYON
BATTLE OF SPRINGFIELD, MISSOURI
(August, 1861)

Some hearts there are of deeper sort,
   Prophetic, sad,
Which yet for cause are trebly clad;
   Known death they fly on:
This wizard-heart and heart-of-oak had Lyon.

"They are more than twenty thousand strong,
   We less than five,
Too few with such a host to strive."
   "Such counsel, fie on!
'Tis battle, or 'tis shame;" and firm stood Lyon.

"For help at need in vain we wait—
   Retreat or fight:
Retreat the foe would take for flight,
   And each proud scion
Feel more elate; the end must come," said Lyon.

By candlelight he wrote the will,
   And left his all
To Her for whom 'twas not enough to fall;
   Loud neighed Orion
Without the tent; drums beat; we marched with Lyon.

The night-tramp done, we spied the Vale
   With guard-fires lit;
Day broke, but trooping clouds made gloom of it:
   "A field to die on,"
Presaged in his unfaltering heart, brave Lyon.

We fought on the grass, we bled in the corn—
   Fate seemed malign;
His horse the Leader led along the line—
   Star-browed Orion;
Bitterly fearless, he rallied us there, brave Lyon.

There came a sound like the slitting of air
   By a swift sharp sword—
A rush of the sound; and the sleek chest broad
   Of black Orion
Heaved, and was fixed; the dead mane waved toward Lyon.

"General, you're hurt—this sleet of balls!"
    He seemed half spent;
With moody and bloody brow, he lowly bent:
    "The field to die on;
But not—not yet; the day is long," breathed Lyon.

For a time becharmed there fell a lull
    In the heart of the fight;
The tree-tops nod, the slain sleep light;
    Warm noon-winds sigh on,
And thoughts which he never spake had Lyon.

Texans and Indians trim for a charge:
    "Stand ready, men!
Let them come close, right up, and then
    After the lead, the iron;
Fire, and charge back!" So strength returned to Lyon.

The Iowa men who held the van,
    Half drilled, were new
To battle: "Some one lead us, then we'll do,"
    Said Corporal Tryon:
"Men! *I* will lead," and a light glared in Lyon.

On they came: they yelped, and fired;
    His spirit sped;
We levelled right in, and the half-breeds fled,
    Nor stayed the iron,
Nor captured the crimson corse of Lyon.

This seer foresaw his soldier-doom,
    Yet willed the fight.
He never turned; his only flight
    Was up to Zion,
Where prophets now and armies greet brave Lyon.

BALL'S BLUFF
A REVERIE
(October, 1861)

One noonday, at my window in the town,
  I saw a sight—saddest that eyes can see—
  Young soldiers marching lustily
      Unto the wars,
With fifes, and flags in mottoed pageantry;
      While all the porches, walks, and doors
Were rich with ladies cheering royally.

They moved like Juny morning on the wave,
  Their hearts were fresh as clover in its prime
  (It was the breezy summer time),
      Life throbbed so strong,
How should they dream that Death in a rosy clime
      Would come to thin their shining throng?
Youth feels immortal, like the gods sublime.

Weeks passed; and at my window, leaving bed,
  By night I mused, of easeful sleep bereft,
  On those brave boys (Ah War! thy theft);
      Some marching feet
Found pause at last by cliffs Potomac cleft;
      Wakeful I mused, while in the street
Far footfalls died away till none were left.

DUPONT'S ROUND FIGHT
(November, 1861)

In time and measure perfect moves
  All Art whose aim is sure;
Evolving rhyme and stars divine
  Have rules, and they endure.

Nor less the Fleet that warred for Right,
  And, warring so, prevailed,
In geometric beauty curved,
  And in an orbit sailed.

The rebel at Port Royal felt
  The Unity overawe,
And rued the spell. A type was here,
  And victory of LAW.

THE STONE FLEET[b]
AN OLD SAILOR'S LAMENT
(December, 1861)

I have a feeling for those ships,
  Each worn and ancient one,
With great bluff bows, and broad in the beam:
  Ay, it was unkindly done.
        But so they serve the Obsolete—
        Even so, Stone Fleet!

You'll say I'm doting; do but think
  I scudded round the Horn in one—
The Tenedos, a glorious
  Good old craft as ever run—
        Sunk (how all unmeet!)
        With the Old Stone Fleet.

An India ship of fame was she,
  Spices and shawls and fans she bore;
A whaler when her wrinkles came—
  Turned off! till, spent and poor,
          Her bones were sold (escheat)!
          Ah! Stone Fleet.

Four were erst patrician keels
  (Names attest what families be),
The Kensington, and Richmond too,
  Leonidas, and Lee:
          But now they have their seat
          With the Old Stone Fleet.

To scuttle them—a pirate deed—
  Sack them, and dismast;
They sunk so slow, they died so hard,
  But gurgling dropped at last.
          Their ghosts in gales repeat
          Woe's us, Stone Fleet!

And all for naught. The waters pass—
  Currents will have their way;
Nature is nobody's ally; 'tis well;
  The harbor is bettered—will stay.
          A failure, and complete,
          Was your Old Stone Fleet.

DONELSON
(February, 1862)

The bitter cup
  Of that hard countermand
Which gave the Envoys up,
Still was wormwood in the mouth,
  And clouds involved the land,
When, pelted by sleet in the icy street,

About the bulletin-board a band
Of eager, anxious people met,
And every wakeful heart was set
On latest news from West or South.
"No seeing here," cries one—"don't crowd"—
"You tall man, pray you, read aloud."

IMPORTANT.

We learn that General Grant,
Marching from Henry overland,
And joined by a force up the Cumberland sent
(Some thirty thousand the command),
On Wednesday a good position won—
Began the siege of Donelson.

This stronghold crowns a river-bluff,
A good broad mile of leveled top;
Inland the ground rolls off
Deep-gorged, and rocky, and broken up—
A wilderness of trees and brush.
The spaded summit shows the roods
Of fixed entrenchments in their hush;
Breast-works and rifle-pits in woods
Perplex the base.—
The welcome weather
Is clear and mild; 'tis much like May.
The ancient boughs that lace together
Along the stream, and hang far forth,
Strange with green mistletoe, betray
A dreamy contrast to the North.

Our troops are full of spirits—say
The siege won't prove a creeping one.
They purpose not the lingering stay
Of old beleaguerers; not that way;
But, full of vim *from Western prairies won,*
They'll make, ere long, a dash at Donelson.

Washed by the storm till the paper grew
Every shade of a streaky blue,

That bulletin stood. The next day brought
A second.

LATER FROM THE FORT.

Grant's investment is complete—
  A semicircular one.
Both wings the Cumberland's margin meet,
Then, backward curving, clasp the rebel seat.
  On Wednesday this good work was done;
  But of the doers some lie prone.
Each wood, each hill, each glen was fought for;
The bold inclosing line we wrought for
Flamed with sharpshooters. Each cliff cost
A limb or life. But back we forced
Reserves and all; made good our hold;
And so we rest.

                    Events unfold.
On Thursday added ground was won,
  A long bold steep: we near the Den.
Later the foe came shouting down
  In sortie, which was quelled; and then
We stormed them on their left.
A chilly change in the afternoon;
The sky, late clear, is now bereft
Of sun. Last night the ground froze hard—
Rings to the enemy as they run
Within their works. A ramrod bites
The lip it meets. The cold incites
To swinging of arms with brisk rebound.
Smart blows 'gainst lusty chests resound.

  Along the outer line we ward
    A crackle of skirmishing goes on.
  Our lads creep round on hand and knee,
  They fight from behind each trunk and stone;
    And sometimes, flying for refuge, one
  Finds 'tis an enemy shares the tree.
  Some scores are maimed by boughs shot off
    In the glades by the Fort's big gun.

We mourn the loss of Colonel Morrison,
  Killed while cheering his regiment on.
Their far sharpshooters try our stuff;
And ours return them puff for puff:
'Tis diamond-cutting-diamond work.
  Woe on the rebel cannoneer
Who shows his head. Our fellows lurk
  Like Indians that waylay the deer
By the wild salt-spring.—The sky is dun,
Foredooming the fall of Donelson.
Stern weather is all unwonted here.
  The people of the country own
We brought it. Yea, the earnest North
Has elementally issued forth
  To storm this Donelson.

FURTHER.

    A yelling rout
Of ragamuffins broke profuse
  To-day from out the Fort.
  Sole uniform they wore, a sort
Of patch, or white badge (as you choose)
  Upon the arm. But leading these,
Or mingling, were men of face
And bearing of patrician race,
Splendid in courage and gold lace—
  The officers. Before the breeze
Made by their charge, down went our line;
But, rallying, charged back in force,
And broke the sally; yet with loss.
This on the left; upon the right
Meanwhile there was an answering fight;
  Assailants and assailed reversed.
The charge too upward, and not down—
Up a steep ridge-side, toward its crown,
  A strong redoubt. But they who first
Gained the fort's base, and marked the trees
Felled, heaped in horned perplexities,
  And shagged with brush; and swarming there
Fierce wasps whose sting was present death—

They faltered, drawing bated breath,
  And felt it was in vain to dare;
Yet still, perforce, returned the ball,
Firing into the tangled wall
Till ordered to come down. They came;
But left some comrades in their fame,
Red on the ridge in icy wreath
And hanging gardens of cold Death.
  But not quite unavenged these fell;
Our ranks once out of range, a blast
  Of shrapnel and quick shell
Burst on the rebel horde, still massed,
  Scattering them pell-mell.
    (This fighting—judging what we read—
    Both charge and countercharge,
    Would seem but Thursday's told at large,
    Before in brief reported.—Ed.)
Night closed in about the Den
  Murky and lowering. Ere long, chill rains.
A night not soon to be forgot,
  Reviving old rheumatic pains
And longings for a cot.
  No blankets, overcoats, or tents.
Coats thrown aside on the warm march here—
We looked not then for changeful cheer;
Tents, coats, and blankets too much care.
  No fires; a fire a mark presents;
  Near by, the trees show bullet-dents.
Rations were eaten cold and raw.
  The men well soaked, came snow; and more—
A midnight sally. Small sleeping done—
    But such is war;
No matter, we'll have Fort Donelson.

       "Ugh! ugh!
'Twill drag along—drag along,"
Growled a cross patriot in the throng,
His battered umbrella like an ambulance-cover
Riddled with bullet-holes, spattered all over.
"Hurrah for Grant!" cried a stripling shrill;

Three urchins joined him with a will,
And some of taller stature cheered.
Meantime a Copperhead passed; he sneered.
  "Win or lose," he pausing said,
"Caps fly the same; all boys, mere boys;
Any thing to make a noise.
  Like to see the list of the dead;
These 'craven Southerners' hold out;
Ay, ay, they'll give you many a bout."
  "We'll beat in the end, sir,"
Firmly said one in staid rebuke,
A solid merchant, square and stout.
  "And do you think it? that way tend, sir?"
Asked the lean Copperhead, with a look
Of splenetic pity. "Yes, I do."
His yellow death's head the croaker shook:
"The country's ruined, that I know."
A shower of broken ice and snow,
  In lieu of words, confuted him;
They saw him hustled round the corner go,
  And each by-stander said—Well suited him.

Next day another crowd was seen
In the dark weather's sleety spleen.
Bald-headed to the storm came out
A man, who, 'mid a joyous shout,
Silently posted this brief sheet:

> GLORIOUS VICTORY OF THE FLEET!
>
> FRIDAY'S GREAT EVENT!
>
> THE ENEMY'S WATER-BATTERIES BEAT!
>
> WE SILENCED EVERY GUN!
>
> THE OLD COMMODORE'S COMPLIMENTS SENT
> PLUMP INTO DONELSON!

"Well, well, go on!" exclaimed the crowd
To him who thus much read aloud.
"That's all," he said. "What! nothing more?"

"Enough for a cheer, though—hip, hurrah!
"But here's old Baldy come again—
"More news!"—And now a different strain.

(Our own reporter a dispatch compiles,
As best he may, from varied sources.)

Large re-enforcements have arrived—
Munitions, men, and horses—
For Grant, and all debarked, with stores.

The enemy's field-works extend six miles—
The gate still hid; so well contrived.

Yesterday stung us; frozen shores
Snow-clad, and through the drear defiles
And over the desolate ridges blew
A Lapland wind.
                    The main affair
Was a good two hours' steady fight
Between our gun-boats and the Fort.
    The Louisville's wheel was smashed outright.
A hundred-and-twenty-eight-pound ball
Came planet-like through a starboard port,
Killing three men, and wounding all
The rest of that gun's crew,
(The captain of the gun was cut in two);
Then splintering and ripping went—
Nothing could be its continent.
    In the narrow stream the Louisville,
Unhelmed, grew lawless, swung around,
    And would have thumped and drifted, till
All the fleet was driven aground,
But for the timely order to retire.

Some damage from our fire, 'tis thought,
Was done the water-batteries of the Fort.

Little else took place that day,
    Except the field artillery in line
Would now and then—for love, they say—
        Exchange a valentine.
The old sharpshooting going on.

Some plan afoot as yet unknown;
So Friday closed round Donelson.

LATER.

 Great suffering through the night—
A stinging one. Our heedless boys
 Were nipped like blossoms. Some dozen
 Hapless wounded men were frozen.
During day being stuck down out of sight,
And help-cries drowned in roaring noise,
They were left just where the skirmish shifted—
Left in dense underbrush snow-drifted.
Some, seeking to crawl in crippled plight,
So stiffened—perished
    Yet in spite
Of pangs for these, no heart is lost.
Hungry, and clothing stiff with frost,
Our men declare a nearing sun
Shall see the fall of Donelson.
 And this they say, yet not disown
The dark redoubts round Donelson,
 And ice-glazed corpses, each a stone—
  A sacrifice to Donelson;
They swear it, and swerve not, gazing on
A flag, deemed black, flying from Donelson.

Some of the wounded in the wood
 Were cared for by the foe last night,
Though he could do them little needed good,
 Himself being all in shivering plight.
The rebel is wrong, but human yet;
He's got a heart, and thrusts a bayonet.
He gives us battle with wondrous will—
This bluff's a perverted Bunker Hill.

The stillness stealing through the throng
The silent thought and dismal fear revealed;
  They turned and went,
  Musing on right and wrong
  And mysteries dimly sealed—

Breasting the storm in daring discontent;
The storm, whose black flag showed in heaven,
As if to say no quarter there was given
    To wounded men in wood,
  Or true hearts yearning for the good—
All fatherless seemed the human soul.
But next day brought a bitterer bowl—
  On the bulletin-board this stood:

Saturday morning at 3 A.M.
    A stir within the Fort betrayed
That the rebels were getting under arms;
    Some plot these early birds had laid.
But a lancing sleet cut him who stared
Into the storm. After some vague alarms,
Which left our lads unscared,
Out sallied the enemy at dim of dawn,
      With cavalry and artillery, and went
      In fury at our environment.
Under cover of shot and shell
    Three columns of infantry rolled on,
    Vomited out of Donelson—
Rolled down the slopes like rivers of hell,
    Surged at our line, and swelled and poured
Like breaking surf. But unsubmerged
      Our men stood up, except where roared
The enemy through one gap. We urged
Our all of manhood to the stress,
But still showed shattered in our desperateness.
    Back set the tide,
But soon afresh rolled in;
  And so it swayed from side to side—
Far batteries joining in the din,
Though sharing in another fray—
  Till all became an Indian fight,
Intricate, dusky, stretching far away,
Yet not without spontaneous plan
  However tangled showed the plight:
Duels all over 'tween man and man,
Duels on cliff-side, and down in ravine,
  Duels at long range, and bone to bone;
Duels every where flitting and half unseen.

Only by courage good as their own,
And strength outlasting theirs,
    Did our boys at last drive the rebels off.
Yet they went not back to their distant lairs
    In strong-hold, but loud in scoff
Maintained themselves on conquered ground—
Uplands; built works, or stalked around.
Our night wing bore this onset. Noon
Brought calm to Donelson.

The reader ceased; the storm beat hard;
    'Twas day, but the office-gas was lit;
    Nature retained her sulking-fit,
        In her hand the shard.

Flitting faces took the hue
Of that washed bulletin-board in view,
And seemed to bear the public grief
As private, and uncertain of relief;
Yea, many an earnest heart was won,
    As broodingly he plodded on,
To find in himself some bitter thing,
Some hardness in his lot as harrowing
        As Donelson.
That night the board stood barren there,
    Oft eyed by wistful people passing,
    Who nothing saw but the rain-beads chasing
Each other down the wafered square,
As down some storm-beat grave-yard stone.
But next day showed—

MORE NEWS LAST NIGHT.

STORY OF SATURDAY AFTERNOON.

VICISSITUDES OF THE WAR.

The damaged gun-boats can't wage fight
For days; so says the Commodore.
Thus no diversion can be had.
Under a sunless sky of lead
    Our grim-faced boys in blackened plight
Gaze toward the ground they held before,
And then on Grant. He marks their mood,

And hails it, and will turn the same to good.
Spite all that they have undergone,
Their desperate hearts are set upon
This winter fort, this stubborn fort,
This castle of the last resort,
        This Donelson.

1 P.M.
                    An order given
        Requires withdrawal from the front
        Of regiments that bore the brunt
Of morning's fray. Their ranks all riven
Are being replaced by fresh, strong men.
Great vigilance in the foeman's Den;
He snuffs the stormers. Need it is
That for that fell assault of his,
That rout inflicted, and self-scorn—
Immoderate in noble natures, torn
By sense of being through slackness overborne—
The rebel be given a quick return:
The kindest face looks now half stern.
Balked of their prey in airs that freeze,
Some fierce ones glare like savages.
And yet, and yet, strange moments are—
Well—blood, and tears, and anguished War!
The morning's battle-ground is seen
        In lifted glades, like meadows rare;
        The blood-drops on the snow-crust there
Like clover in the white-weed show—
        Flushed fields of death, that call again—
        Call to our men, and not in vain,
For that way must the stormers go.

3 P.M.
                The work begins.
Light drifts of men thrown forward, fade
        In skirmish-line along the slope,
Where some dislodgments must be made
        Ere the stormer with the strong-hold cope.

Lew Wallace, moving to retake
The heights late lost—
                    (Herewith a break.

Storms at the West derange the wires.
Doubtless, ere morning, we shall hear
The end; we look for news to cheer—
  Let Hope fan all her fires.)

Next day in large bold hand was seen
The closing bulletin:

VICTORY!

        Our troops have retrieved the day
By one grand surge along the line;
The spirit that urged them was divine.
    The first works flooded, naught could stay
The stormers: on! still on!
Bayonets for Donelson!
Over the ground that morning lost
Rolled the blue billows, tempest-tossed,
    Following a hat on the point of a sword.
Spite shell and round-shot, grape and canister,
Up they climbed without rail or banister
    Up the steep hill-sides long and broad,
Driving the rebel deep within his works.
'Tis nightfall; not an enemy lurks.
    In sight. The chafing men
      Fret for more fight:
    "To-night, to-night let us take the Den!"
But night is treacherous, Grant is wary;
Of brave blood be a little chary.
Patience! The Fort is good as won;
To-morrow, and into Donelson.

LATER AND LAST.

THE FORT IS OURS.

    A flag came out at early morn
Bringing surrender. From their towers
    Floats out the banner late their scorn.
In Dover, hut and house are full
      Of rebels dead or dying.
    The National flag is flying
From the crammed court-house pinnacle.

Great boat-loads of our wounded go
To-day to Nashville. The sleet-winds blow;
But all is right: the fight is won,
The winter-fight for Donelson.
        Hurrah!
The spell of old defeat is broke,
   The habit of victory begun;
Grant strikes the war's first sounding stroke
        At Donelson.
For lists of killed and wounded, see
The morrow's dispatch: to-day 'tis victory.

The man who read this to the crowd
   Shouted as the end he gained;
     And though the unflagging tempest rained,
       They answered him aloud.
And hand grasped hand, and glances met
In happy triumph; eyes grew wet.
O, to the punches brewed that night
Went little water. Windows bright
Beamed rosy on the sleet without,
And from the deep street came the frequent shout;
While some in prayer, as these in glee,
Blessed heaven for the winter-victory.
But others were who wakeful laid
   In midnight beds, and early rose,
     And, feverish in the foggy snows,
Snatched the damp paper—wife and maid.
   The death-list like a river flows
     Down the pale sheet,
And there the whelming waters meet.

  Ah God! may Time with happy haste
  Bring wail and triumph to a waste,
    And war be done;
  The battle flag-staff fall athwart
  The curs'd ravine, and wither; naught
    Be left of trench or gun;
  The bastion, let it ebb away,
  Washed with the river bed; and Day
    In vain seek Donelson.

THE CUMBERLAND
(March, 1862)

Some names there are of telling sound,
  Whose voweled syllables free
Are pledge that they shall ever live renowned;
    Such seems to be
A Frigate's name (by present glory spanned)—
  The Cumberland.

        Sounding name as ere was sung,
        Flowing, rolling on the tongue—
        Cumberland! Cumberland!

She warred and sunk. There's no denying
  That she was ended—quelled;
And yet her flag above her fate is flying,
    As when it swelled
Unswallowed by the swallowing sea: so grand—
  The Cumberland.

        Goodly name as ere was sung,
        Roundly rolling on the tongue—
        Cumberland! Cumberland!

What need to tell how she was fought—
  The sinking flaming gun—
The gunner leaping out the port—
  Washed back, undone!
Her dead unconquerably manned
  The Cumberland.

        Noble name as ere was sung,
        Slowly roll it on the tongue—
        Cumberland! Cumberland!

Long as hearts shall share the flame
  Which burned in that brave crew,
Her fame shall live—outlive the victor's name;
    For this is due.
Your flag and flag-staff shall in story stand—
  Cumberland!

        Sounding name as ere was sung,
        Long they'll roll it on the tongue—
        Cumberland! Cumberland!

IN THE TURRET
(March, 1862)

Your honest heart of duty, Worden,
  So helped you that in fame you dwell;
Your bore the first iron battle's burden
  Sealed as in a diving-bell.
Alcides, groping into haunted hell
To bring forth King Admetus' bride,
Braved naught more vaguely direful and untried.
  What poet shall uplift his charm,
Bold Sailor, to your height of daring,
  And interblend therewith the calm,
And build a goodly style upon your bearing.

Escaped the gale of outer ocean—
  Cribbed in a craft which like a log
Was washed by every billow's motion—
  By night you heard of Og
The huge; nor felt your courage clog
At tokens of his onset grim:
You marked the sunk ship's flag-staff slim,
  Lit by her burning sister's heart;
You marked, and mused: "Day brings the trial:
  Then be it proved if I have part
With men whose manhood never took denial."

A prayer went up—a champion's. Morning
  Beheld you in the Turret walled
By adamant, where a spirit forewarning
  And all-deriding called:
"Man, darest thou—desperate, unappalled—
Be first to lock thee in the armored tower?
I have thee now; and what the battle-hour
  To me shall bring—heed well—thou'lt share;
This plot-work, planned to be the foeman's terror,
  To thee may prove a goblin-snare;
Its very strength and cunning—monstrous error!"

"Stand up, my heart; be strong; what matter
  If here thou seest thy welded tomb?
And let huge Og with thunders batter—
  Duty be still my doom,

Though drowning come in liquid gloom;
First duty, duty next, and duty last;
Ay, Turret, rivet me here to duty fast!"—
  So nerved, you fought, wisely and well;
And live, twice live in life and story;
  But over your Monitor dirges swell,
In wind and wave that keep the rites of glory.

THE TEMERAIRE[c]

(SUPPOSED TO HAVE BEEN SUGGESTED TO AN ENGLISHMAN OF THE OLD ORDER BY THE FIGHT OF THE MONITOR AND MERRIMAC)

The gloomy hulls, in armor grim,
  Like clouds o'er moors have met,
And prove that oak, and iron, and man
  Are tough in fibre yet.

But Splendors wane. The sea-fight yields
  No front of old display;
The garniture, emblazonment,
  And heraldry all decay.

Towering afar in parting light,
  The fleets like Albion's forelands shine—
The full-sailed fleets, the shrouded show
  Of Ships-of-the-Line.

The fighting Temeraire,
  Built of a thousand trees,
Lunging out her lightnings,
  And beetling o'er the seas—
O Ship, how brave and fair,
  That fought so oft and well,
On open decks you manned the gun
  Armorial.
What cheerings did you share,
  Impulsive in the van,
When down upon leagued France and
      Spain
    We English ran—

The freshet at your bowsprit
  Like the foam upon the can.
Bickering, your colors
  Licked up the Spanish air,
You flapped with flames of battle-flags—
  Your challenge, Temeraire!
The rear ones of your fleet
  They yearned to share your place,
Still vying with the Victory
  Throughout that earnest race—
The Victory, whose Admiral,
  With orders nobly won,
Shone in the globe of the battle glow—
  The angel in that sun.
Parallel in story,
  Lo, the stately pair,
As late in grapple ranging,
  The foe between them there—
When four great hulls lay tiered,
  And the fiery tempest cleared,
And your prizes twain appeared,
      Temeraire!

But Trafalgar is over now,
  The quarter-deck undone;
The carved and castled navies fire
  Their evening-gun.
O, Titan Temeraire,
  Your stern-lights fade away;
Your bulwarks to the years must yield,
  And heart-of-oak decay.
A pigmy steam-tug tows you,
  Gigantic, to the shore—
Dismantled of your guns and spars,
  And sweeping wings of war.
The rivets clinch the iron-clads,
  Men learn a deadlier lore;
But Fame has nailed your battle-flags—
  Your ghost it sails before:
O, the navies old and oaken,
  O, the Temeraire no more!

A UTILITARIAN VIEW OF THE MONITOR'S FIGHT

Plain be the phrase, yet apt the verse,
  More ponderous than nimble;
For since grimed War here laid aside
His painted pomp, 'twould ill befit
    Overmuch to ply
  The rhyme's barbaric cymbal.

Hail to victory without the gaud
  Of glory; zeal that needs no fans
Of banners; plain mechanic power
Plied cogently in War now placed—
    Where War belongs—
  Among the trades and artisans.

Yet this was battle, and intense—
  Beyond the strife of fleets heroic;
Deadlier, closer, calm 'mid storm;
No passion; all went on by crank,
    Pivot, and screw,
  And calculations of caloric.

Needless to dwell; the story's known.
  The ringing of those plates on plates
Still ringeth round the world—
The clangor of that blacksmith's fray.
    The anvil-din
  Resounds this message from the Fates:

War shall yet be, and to the end;
  But war-paint shows the streaks of weather;
War yet shall be, but warriors
Are now but operatives; War's made
    Less grand than Peace,
  And a singe runs through lace and feather.

SHILOH
A REQUIEM
(April, 1862)

Skimming lightly, wheeling still,
  The swallows fly low
Over the field in clouded days,
  The forest-field of Shiloh—
Over the field where April rain
Solaced the parched ones stretched in pain
Through the pause of night
That followed the Sunday fight
  Around the church of Shiloh—
The church so lone, the log-built one,
That echoed to many a parting groan
    And natural prayer
  Of dying foemen mingled there—
Foemen at morn, but friends at eve—
  Fame or country least their care:
(What like a bullet can undeceive!)
  But now they lie low,
While over them the swallows skim,
  And all is hushed at Shiloh.

THE BATTLE FOR THE MISSISSIPPI
(April, 1862)

When Israel camped by Migdol hoar,
  Down at her feet her shawm she threw,
But Moses sung and timbrels rung
  For Pharaoh's stranded crew.
So God appears in apt events—
  The Lord is a man of war!
So the strong wing to the muse is given
  In victory's roar.

Deep be the ode that hymns the fleet—
  The fight by night—the fray
Which bore our Flag against the powerful stream,
  And led it up to day.
Dully through din of larger strife
  Shall bay that warring gun;
But none the less to us who live
  It peals—an echoing one.

The shock of ships, the jar of walls,
  The rush through thick and thin—
The flaring fire-rafts, glare and gloom—
  Eddies, and shells that spin—
The boom-chain burst, the hulks dislodged,
  The jam of gun-boats driven,
Or fired, or sunk—made up a war
  Like Michael's waged with leven.

The manned Varuna stemmed and quelled
  The odds which hard beset;
The oaken flag-ship, half ablaze,
  Passed on and thundered yet;
While foundering, gloomed in grimy flame,
  The Ram Manassas—hark the yell!—
Plunged, and was gone; in joy or fright,
  The River gave a startled swell.

They fought through lurid dark till dawn;
  The war-smoke rolled away
With clouds of night, and showed the fleet
  In scarred yet firm array,
Above the forts, above the drift
  Of wrecks which strife had made;
And Farragut sailed up to the town
  And anchored—sheathed the blade.

The moody broadsides, brooding deep,
  Hold the lewd mob at bay,
While o'er the armed decks' solemn aisles
  The meek church-pennons play;
By shotted guns the sailors stand,
  With foreheads bound or bare;

The captains and the conquering crews
  Humble their pride in prayer.

They pray; and after victory, prayer
  Is meet for men who mourn their slain;
The living shall unmoor and sail,
  But Death's dark anchor secret deeps detain.
Yet Glory slants her shaft of rays
  Far through the undisturbed abyss;
There must be other, nobler worlds for them
  Who nobly yield their lives in this.

MALVERN HILL
(July, 1862)

Ye elms that wave on Malvern Hill
  In prime of morn and May,
Recall ye how McClellan's men
    Here stood at bay?
While deep within yon forest dim
  Our rigid comrades lay—
Some with the cartridge in their mouth,
Others with fixed arms lifted south—
    Invoking so
The cypress glades? Ah wilds of woe!

The spires of Richmond, late beheld
  Through rifts in musket-haze,
Were closed from view in clouds of dust
    On leaf-walled ways,
Where streamed our wagons in caravan;
  And the Seven Nights and Days
Of march and fast, retreat and fight,
Pinched our grimed faces to ghastly plight—
    Does the elm wood
Recall the haggard beards of blood?

The battle-smoked flag, with stars eclipsed,
  We followed (it never fell!)—

In silence husbanded our strength—
      Received their yell;
Till on this slope we patient turned
   With cannon ordered well;
Reverse we proved was not defeat;
But ah, the sod what thousands meet!—
      Does Malvern Wood
Bethink itself, and muse and brood?

> *We elms of Malvern Hill*
>   *Remember every thing;*
> *But sap the twig will fill;*
> *Wag the world how it will,*
>   *Leaves must be green in Spring.*

THE VICTOR OF ANTIETAM[e]
(1862)

When tempest winnowed grain from bran,
And men were looking for a man,
Authority called you to the van,
      McClellan;
Along the line the plaudit ran,
As later when Antietam's cheers began.

Through storm-cloud and eclipse must move
Each Cause and Man, dear to the stars and Jove;
Nor always can the wisest tell
Deferred fulfillment from the hopeless knell—
The struggler from the floundering ne'er-do-well.
A pall-cloth on the Seven Days fell,
      McClellan—
Unprosperously heroical!
Who could Antietam's wreath foretell?

Authority called you; then, in mist
And loom of jeopardy—dismissed.
But staring peril soon appalled;
You, the Discarded, she recalled—

Recalled you, nor endured delay;
And forth you rode upon a blasted way,
Arrayed Pope's rout, and routed Lee's array,
        McClellan:
Your tent was choked with captured flags that day,
        McClellan.
Antietam was a telling fray.

Recalled you; and she heard your drum
Advancing through the ghastly gloom.
You manned the wall, you propped the Dome,
You stormed the powerful stormer home,
        McClellan:
Antietam's cannon long shall boom.

At Alexandria, left alone,
        McClellan—
Your veterans sent from you, and thrown
To fields and fortunes all unknown—
What thoughts were yours, revealed to none,
While faithful still you labored on—
Hearing the far Manassas gun!
        McClellan,
Only Antietam could atone.

You fought in the front (an evil day,
        McClellan)—
The fore-front of the first assay;
The Cause went sounding, groped its way;
The leadsmen quarrelled in the bay;
Quills thwarted swords; divided sway;
The rebel flushed in his lusty May:
You did your best, as in you lay,
        McClellan.
Antietam's sun-burst sheds a ray.

Your medalled soldiers love you well,
        McClellan:
Name your name, their true hearts swell;
With you they shook dread Stonewall's spell, ͬ
With you they braved the blended yell
Of rebel and maligner fell;

With you in shame or fame they dwell,
    McClellan:
Antietam-braves a brave can tell.

And when your comrades (now so few,
    McClellan—
Such ravage in deep files they rue)
Meet round the board, and sadly view
The empty places; tribute due
They render to the dead—and you!
Absent and silent o'er the blue;
The one-armed lift the wine to *you*,
    McClellan,
And great Antietam's cheers renew.

BATTLE OF STONE RIVER, TENNESSEE
A VIEW FROM OXFORD CLOISTERS
(January, 1863)

With Tewksbury and Barnet heath
  In days to come the field shall blend,
The story dim and date obscure;
  In legend all shall end.
Even now, involved in forest shade
  A Druid-dream the strife appears,
The fray of yesterday assumes
  The haziness of years.
      In North and South still beats the vein
      Of Yorkist and Lancastrian.

Our rival Roses warred for Sway—
  For Sway, but named the name of Right;
And Passion, scorning pain and death,
  Lent sacred fervor to the fight.
Each lifted up a broidered cross,
  While crossing blades profaned the sign;
Monks blessed the fratricidal lance,
  And sisters scarfs could twine.
      Do North and South the sin retain
      Of Yorkist and Lancastrian?

But Rosecrans in the cedarn glade,
  And, deep in denser cypress gloom,
Dark Breckinridge, shall fade away
    Or thinly loom.

The pale throngs who in forest cowed
  Before the spell of battle's pause,
Forefelt the stillness that shall dwell
    On them and on their wars.
        North and South shall join the train
        Of Yorkist and Lancastrian.

But where the sword has plunged so deep,
  And then been turned within the wound
By deadly Hate; where Climes contend
    On vasty ground—
No warning Alps or seas between,
  And small the curb of creed or law,
And blood is quick, and quick the brain;
    Shall North and South their rage deplore,
        And reunited thrive amain
        Like Yorkist and Lancastrian?

RUNNING THE BATTERIES

AS OBSERVED FROM THE ANCHORAGE ABOVE VICKSBURGH
(April, 1863)

A moonless night—a friendly one;
  A haze dimmed the shadowy shore
As the first lampless boat slid silent on;
  Hist! and we spake no more;
We but pointed, and stilly, to what we saw.

We felt the dew, and seemed to feel
  The secret like a burden laid.
The first boat melts; and a second keel
  Is blent with the foliaged shade—
Their midnight rounds have the rebel officers made?

Unspied as yet. A third—a fourth—
    Gunboat and transport in Indian file
Upon the war-path, smooth from the North;
    But the watch may they hope to beguile?
The manned river-batteries stretch for mile on mile.

A flame leaps out; they are seen;
    Another and another gun roars;
We tell the course of the boats through the screen
    By each further fort that pours,
And we guess how they jump from their beds on those
        shrouded shores.

Converging fires. We speak, though low:
    "That blastful furnace can they thread?"
"Why, Shadrach, Meshach, and Abed-nego
    Came out all right, we read;
The Lord, be sure, he helps his people, Ned."

How we strain our gaze. On bluffs they shun
    A golden growing flame appears—
Confirms to a silvery steadfast one:
    "The town is afire!" crows Hugh: "three cheers!"
Lot stops his mouth: "Nay, lad, better three tears."

A purposed light; it shows our fleet;
    Yet a little late in its searching ray,
So far and strong, that in phantom ceat
    Lank on the deck our shadows lay;
The shining flag-ship stings their guns to furious play.

How dread to mark her near the glare
    And glade of death the beacon throws
Athwart the racing waters there;
    One by one each plainer grows,
Then speeds a blazoned target to our gladdened foes.

The impartial cresset lights as well
    The fixed forts to the boats that run;
And, plunged from the ports, their answers swell
    Back to each fortress dun:
Ponderous words speaks every monster gun.

Fearless they flash through gates of flame,
    The salamanders hard to hit,

Though vivid shows each bulky frame;
  And never the batteries intermit,
Nor the boat's huge guns; they fire and flit.

Anon a lull. The beacon dies:
  "Are they out of that strait accurst?"
But other flames now dawning rise,
  Not mellowly brilliant like the first,
But rolled in smoke, whose whitish volumes burst.

A baleful brand, a hurrying torch
  Whereby anew the boats are seen—
A burning transport all alurch!
  Breathless we gaze; yet still we glean
Glimpses of beauty as we eager lean.

The effulgence takes an amber glow
  Which bathes the hill-side villas far;
Affrighted ladies mark the show
  Painting the pale magnolia—
The fair, false, Circe light of cruel War.

The barge drifts doomed, a plague-struck one.
  Shoreward in yawls the sailors fly.
But the gauntlet now is nearly run,
  The spleenful forts by fits reply,
And the burning boat dies down in morning's sky.

All out of range. Adieu, Messieurs!
  Jeers, as it speeds, our parting gun.
So burst we through their barriers
  And menaces every one:
So Porter proves himself a brave man's son.[g]

STONEWALL JACKSON
MORTALLY WOUNDED AT CHANCELLORSVILLE
(May, 1863)

The Man who fiercest charged in fight,
  Whose sword and prayer were long—
      Stonewall!
Even him who stoutly stood for Wrong,
How can we praise? Yet coming days
  Shall not forget him with this song.

Dead is the Man whose Cause is dead,
  Vainly he died and set his seal—
      Stonewall!
Earnest in error, as we feel;
True to the thing he deemed was due,
  True as John Brown or steel.

Relentlessly he routed us;
  But *we* relent, for he is low—
      Stonewall!
Justly his fame we outlaw; so
We drop a tear on the bold Virginian's bier,
  Because no wreath we owe.

STONEWALL JACKSON
(ASCRIBED TO A VIRGINIAN)

One man we claim of wrought renown
  Which not the North shall care to slur;
A Modern lived who sleeps in death,
  Calm as the marble Ancients are:
    'Tis he whose life, though a vapor's wreath,
    Was charged with the lightning's burning breath—
    Stonewall, stormer of the war.

But who shall hymn the Roman heart?
  A stoic he, but even more:

The iron will and lion thew
  Were strong to inflict as to endure:
    Who like him could stand, or pursue?
    His fate the fatalist followed through:
    In all his great soul found to do
      Stonewall followed his star.

He followed his star on the Romney march
  Through the sleet to the wintry war;
And he followed it on when he bowed the grain—
  The Wind of the Shenandoah;
    At Gaines's Mill in the giants' strain—
    On the fierce forced stride to Manassas-plain,
    Where his sword with thunder was clothed again,
      Stonewall followed his star.

His star he followed athwart the flood
  To Potomac's Northern shore,
When midway wading, his host of braves
  "My Maryland!" loud did roar—
    To red Antietam's field of graves,
    Through mountain-passes, woods and waves,
    They followed their pagod with hymns and glaives,
      For Stonewall followed a star.

Back it led him to Marye's slope,
  Where the shock and the fame he bore;
And to green Moss-Neck it guided him—
  Brief respite from throes of war:
    To the laurel glade by the Wilderness grim,
    Through climaxed victory naught shall dim,
    Even unto death it piloted him—
      Stonewall followed his star.

Its lead he followed in gentle ways
  Which never the valiant mar;
A cap we sent him, bestarred, to replace
  The sun-scorched helm of war:
    A fillet he made of the shining lace
    Childhood's laughing brow to grace—
      Not his was a goldsmith's star.

O, much of doubt in after days
  Shall cling, as now, to the war;

Of the right and the wrong they'll still debate,
  Puzzled by Stonewall's star:
     "Fortune went with the North elate,"
    "Ay, but the South had Stonewall's weight,
     And he fell in the South's vain war."

GETTYSBURG
THE CHECK
(July, 1863)

A pride of the days in prime of the months
  Now trebled in great renown,
When before the ark of our holy cause
    Fell Dagon down—
Dagon foredoomed, who, armed and targed,
Never his impious heart enlarged
Beyond that hour; God walled his power,
And there the last invader charged.

He charged, and in that charge condensed
  His all of hate and all of fire;
He sought to blast us in his scorn,
    And wither us in his ire.
Before him went the shriek of shells—
Aerial screamings, taunts and yells;
Then the three waves in flashed advance
  Surged, but were met, and back they set:
Pride was repelled by sterner pride,
  And Right is a strong-hold yet.

Before our lines it seemed a beach
  Which wild September gales have strown
With havoc on wreck, and dashed therewith
    Pale crews unknown—
Men, arms, and steeds. The evening sun
Died on the face of each lifeless one,
And died along the winding marge of fight
    And searching-parties lone.

Sloped on the hill the mounds were green,
  Our centre held that place of graves,

And some still hold it in their swoon,
  And over these a glory waves.
The warrior-monument, crashed in fight,[h]
Shall soar transfigured in loftier light,
    A meaning ampler bear;
Soldier and priest with hymn and prayer
Have laid the stone, and every bone
    Shall rest in honor there.

THE HOUSE-TOP
A NIGHT PIECE
(July, 1863)

No sleep. The sultriness pervades the air
And binds the brain—a dense oppression, such
As tawny tigers feel in matted shades,
Vexing their blood and making apt for ravage.
Beneath the stars the roofy desert spreads
Vacant as Libya. All is hushed near by.
Yet fitfully from far breaks a mixed surf
Of muffled sound, the Atheist roar of riot.
Yonder, where parching Sirius set in drought,
Balefully glares red Arson—there—and there.
The Town is taken by its rats—ship-rats
And rats of the wharves. All civil charms
And priestly spells which late held hearts in awe—
Fear-bound, subjected to a better sway
Than sway of self; these like a dream dissolve,
And man rebounds whole aeons back in nature.[i]
Hail to the low dull rumble, dull and dead,
And ponderous drag that shakes the wall.
Wise Draco comes, deep in the midnight roll
Of black artillery; he comes, though late;
In code corroborating Calvin's creed
And cynic tyrannies of honest kings;
He comes, nor parlies; and the Town, redeemed,
Gives thanks devout; nor, being thankful, heeds
The grimy slur on the Republic's faith implied,
Which holds that Man is naturally good,
And—more—is Nature's Roman, never to be scourged.

LOOK-OUT MOUNTAIN
THE NIGHT FIGHT
(November, 1863)

Who inhabiteth the Mountain
  That it shines in lurid light,
And is rolled about with thunders,
  And terrors, and a blight,
Like Kaf the peak of Eblis—
  Kaf, the evil height?
Who has gone up with a shouting
  And a trumpet in the night?

There is battle in the Mountain—
  Might assaulteth Might;
'Tis the fastness of the Anarch,
  Torrent-torn, an ancient height;
The crags resound the clangor
  Of the war of Wrong and Right;
And the armies in the valley
  Watch and pray for dawning light.

Joy, joy, the day is breaking,
  And the cloud is rolled from sight;
There is triumph in the Morning
For the Anarch's plunging flight;
God has glorified the Mountain
  Where a Banner burneth bright,
And the armies in the valley
  They are fortified in right.

CHATTANOOGA
(November, 1863)

A kindling impulse seized the host
  Inspired by Heaven's elastic air;[1]
Their hearts outran their General's plan,
  Though Grant commanded there—
Grant, who without reserve can dare;

And, "Well, go on and do your will,"
    He said, and measured the mountain then:
So master-riders fling the rein—
    But you must know your men.

On yester-morn in grayish mist,
    Armies like ghosts on hills had fought,
And rolled from the cloud their thunders loud
    The Cumberlands far had caught:
    To-day the sunlit steeps are sought.
Grant stood on cliffs whence all was plain,
    And smoked as one who feels no cares;
But mastered nervousness intense
    Alone such calmness wears.

The summit-cannon plunge their flame
    Sheer down the primal wall,
But up and up each linking troop
    In stretching festoons crawl—
    Nor fire a shot. Such men appall
The foe, though brave. He, from the brink,
    Looks far along the breadth of slope,
And sees two miles of dark dots creep,
    And knows they mean the cope.

He sees them creep. Yet here and there
    Half hid 'mid leafless groves they go;
As men who ply through traceries high
    Of turreted marbles show—
    So dwindle these to eyes below.
But fronting shot and flanking shell
    Sliver and rive the inwoven ways;
High tops of oaks and high hearts fall,
But never the climbing stays.

From right to left, from left to right
    They roll the rallying cheer—
Vie with each other, brother with brother,
    Who shall the first appear—
    What color-bearer with colors clear
In sharp relief, like sky-drawn Grant,
    Whose cigar must now be near the stump—

While in solicitude his back
  Heaps slowly to a hump.

Near and more near; till now the flags
  Run like a catching flame;
And one flares highest, to peril nighest—
  He means to make a name:
Salvos! they give him his fame.
The staff is caught, and next the rush,
  And then the leap where death has led;
Flag answered flag along the crest,
  And swarms of rebels fled.

But some who gained the envied Alp,
  And—eager, ardent, earnest there—
Dropped into Death's wide-open arms,
  Quelled on the wing like eagles struck in air—
  Forever they slumber young and fair,
The smile upon them as they died;
  Their end attained, that end a height:
Life was to these a dream fulfilled,
  And death a starry night.

THE ARMIES OF THE WILDERNESS
(1863-4)

I

Like snows the camps on Southern hills
  Lay all the winter long,
Our levies there in patience stood—
  They stood in patience strong.
On fronting slopes gleamed other camps
  Where faith as firmly clung:
Ah, froward kin! so brave amiss—
  The zealots of the Wrong.

    In this strife of brothers
     (God, hear their country call),

However it be, whatever betide,
Let not the just one fall.

Through the pointed glass our soldiers saw
  The base-ball bounding sent:
They could have joined them in their sport
  But for the vale's deep rent.
And others turned the reddish soil,
  Like diggers of graves they bent;
The reddish soil and trenching toil
  Begat presentiment.

> *Did the Fathers feel mistrust?*
>   *Can no final good be wrought?*
> *Over and over, again and again*
>   *Must the fight for the Right be fought?*

They lead a Gray-back to the crag:
  "Your earth-works yonder—tell us, man!"
"A prisoner—no deserter, I,
  Nor one of the tell-tale clan."
His rags they mark: "True-blue like you
  Should wear the color—your Country's, man!"
He grinds his teeth: "However that be,
  Yon earth-works have their plan."

> *Such brave ones, foully snared*
>   *By Belial's wily plea,*
> *Were faithful unto the evil end—*
>   *Feudal fidelity.*

"Well, then, your camps—come, tell the names!"
  Freely he leveled his finger then:
"Yonder—see—are our Georgians; on the crest,
  The Carolinians; lower, past the glen,
Virginians—Alabamians—Mississippians—Kentuckians
  (Follow my finger)—Tennesseans; and the ten
Camps *there*—ask your grave-pits; they'll tell.
  Halloa! I see the picket-hut, the den
Where I last night lay." "Where's Lee?"
  "In the hearts and bayonets of all yon men!"

> *The tribes swarm up to war*
>   *As in ages long ago,*

> *Ere the palm of promise leaved*
> *And the lily of Christ did blow.*

Their mounted pickets for miles are spied
  Dotting the lowland plain,
The nearer ones in their veteran-rags—
  Loutish they loll in lazy disdain.
But ours in perilous places bide
  With rifles ready and eyes that strain
Deep through the dim suspected wood
  Where the Rapidan rolls amain.

> *The Indian has passed away,*
> *But creeping comes another—*
> *Deadlier far. Picket,*
> *Take heed—take heed of thy brother!*

From a wood-hung height, an outpost lone,
  Crowned with a woodman's fort,
The sentinel looks on a land of dole,
  Like Paran, all amort.
Black chimneys, gigantic in moor-like wastes,
  The scowl of the clouded sky retort;
The hearth is a houseless stone again—
  Ah! where shall the people be sought?

> *Since the venom such blastment deals,*
> *The South should have paused, and thrice,*
> *Ere with heat of her hate she hatched*
> *The egg with the cockatrice.*

A path down the mountain winds to the glade
  Where the dead of the Moonlight Fight lie low;
A hand reaches out of the thin-laid mould
  As begging help which none can bestow.
But the field-mouse small and busy ant
  Heap their hillocks, to hide if they may the woe:
By the bubbling spring lies the rusted canteen,
  And the drum which the drummer-boy dying let go.

> *Dust to dust, and blood for blood—*
> *Passion and pangs! Has Time*
> *Gone back? or is this the Age*
> *Of the world's great Prime?*

The wagon mired and cannon dragged
  Have trenched their scar; the plain
Tramped like the cindery beach of the damned—
  A site for the city of Cain.
And stumps of forests for dreary leagues
  Like a massacre show. The armies have lain
By fires where gums and balms did burn,
  And the seeds of Summer's reign.

> *Where are the birds and boys?*
>   *Who shall go chestnutting when*
> *October returns? The nuts—*
>   *O, long ere they grow again.*

They snug their huts with the chapel-pews,
  In court-houses stable their steeds—
Kindle their fires with indentures and bonds,
  And old Lord Halifax's parchment deeds;
And Virginian gentlemen's libraries old—
  Books which only the scholar heeds—
Are flung to his kennel. It is ravage and range,
  And gardens are left to weeds.

> *Turned adrift into war*
>   *Man runs wild on the plain,*
> *Like the jennets let loose*
>   *On the Pampas—zebras again.*

Like the Pleiads dim, see the tents through the storm—
  Aloft by the hill-side hamlet's graves,
On a head-stone used for a hearth-stone there
  The water is bubbling for punch for our braves.
What if the night be drear, and the blast
  Ghostly shrieks? their rollicking staves
Make frolic the heart; beating time with their swords,
  What care they if Winter raves?

> *Is life but a dream? and so,*
>   *In the dream do men laugh aloud?*
> *So strange seems mirth in a camp,*
>   *So like a white tent to a shroud.*

II

The May-weed springs; and comes a Man
    And mounts our Signal Hill;
A quiet Man, and plain in garb—
    Briefly he looks his fill,
Then drops his gray eye on the ground,
    Like a loaded mortar he is still:
Meekness and grimness meet in him—
    The silent General.

> *Were men but strong and wise,*
>   *Honest as Grant, and calm,*
> *War would be left to the red and black ants,*
>   *And the happy world disarm.*

That eve a stir was in the camps,
    Forerunning quiet soon to come
Among the streets of beechen huts
    No more to know the drum.
The weed shall choke the lowly door,
    And foxes peer within the gloom,
Till scared perchance by Mosby's prowling men,
    Who ride in the rear of doom.

> *Far West, and farther South,*
>   *Wherever the sword has been,*
> *Deserted camps are met,*
>   *And desert graves are seen.*

The livelong night they ford the flood;
    With guns held high they silent press,
Till shimmers the grass in their bayonets' sheen—
    On Morning's banks their ranks they dress;
Then by the forests lightly wind,
    Whose waving boughs the pennons seem to bless,
Borne by the cavalry scouting on—
    Sounding the Wilderness.

> *Like shoals of fish in spring*
>   *That visit Crusoe's isle,*

> *The host in the lonesome place—*
> *The hundred thousand file.*

The foe that held his guarded hills
  Must speed to woods afar;
For the scheme that was nursed by the Culpepper hearth
  With the slowly-smoked cigar—
The scheme that smouldered through winter long
  Now bursts into act—into war—
The resolute scheme of a heart as calm
  As the Cyclone's core.

> *The fight for the city is fought*
>   *In Nature's old domain;*
> *Man goes out to the wilds,*
>   *And Orpheus' charm is vain.*

In glades they meet skull after skull
  Where pine-cones lay—the rusted gun,
Green shoes full of bones, the mouldering coat
  And cuddled-up skeleton;
And scores of such. Some start as in dreams,
  And comrades lost bemoan:
By the edge of those wilds Stonewall had charged—
  But the Year and the Man were gone.

> *At the height of their madness*
>   *The night winds pause,*
> *Recollecting themselves;*
>   *But no lull in these wars.*

A gleam!—a volley! And who shall go
  Storming the swarmers in jungles dread?
No cannon-ball answers, no proxies are sent—
  They rush in the shrapnel's stead.
Plume and sash are vanities now—
  Let them deck the pall of the dead;
They go where the shade is, perhaps into Hades,
  Where the brave of all times have led.

> *There's a dust of hurrying feet,*
>   *Bitten lips and bated breath,*
> *And drums that challenge to the grave,*
>   *And faces fixed, forefeeling death.*

What husky huzzahs in the hazy groves—
  What flying encounters fell;
Pursuer and pursued like ghosts disappear
  In gloomed shade—their end who shall tell?
The crippled, a ragged-barked stick for a crutch,
  Limp to some elfin dell—
Hobble from the sight of dead faces—white
  As pebbles in a well.

> *Few burial rites shall be;*
>   *No priest with book and band*
> *Shall come to the secret place*
>   *Of the corpse in the foeman's land.*

Watch and fast, march and fight—clutch your gun!
  Day-fights and night-fights; sore is the stress;
Look, through the pines what line comes on?
  Longstreet slants through the hauntedness!

'Tis charge for charge, and shout for yell:
  Such battles on battles oppress—
But Heaven lent strength, the Right strove well,
  And emerged from the Wilderness.

> *Emerged, for the way was won;*
>   *But the Pillar of Smoke that led*
> *Was brand-like with ghosts that went up*
>   *Ashy and red.*

None can narrate that strife in the pines,
  A seal is on it—Sabæan lore!
Obscure as the wood, the entangled rhyme
  But hints at the maze of war—
Vivid glimpses or livid through peopled gloom,
  And fires which creep and char—
A riddle of death, of which the slain
    Sole solvers are.

> *Long they withhold the roll*
>   *Of the shroudless dead. It is right;*
> *Not yet can we bear the flare*
>   *Of the funeral light.*

ON THE PHOTOGRAPH OF A CORPS COMMANDER

Ay, man is manly. Here you see
  The warrior-carriage of the head,
And brave dilation of the frame;
  And lighting all, the soul that led
In Spottsylvania's charge to victory,
  Which justifies his fame.

A cheering picture. It is good
  To look upon a Chief like this,
In whom the spirit moulds the form.
  Here favoring Nature, oft remiss,
With eagle mien expressive has endued
  A man to kindle strains that warm.

Trace back his lineage, and his sires,
  Yeoman or noble, you shall find
Enrolled with men of Agincourt,
  Heroes who shared great Harry's mind.
Down to us come the knightly Norman fires,
  And front the Templars bore.

Nothing can lift the heart of man
  Like manhood in a fellow-man.
The thought of heaven's great King afar
But humbles us—too weak to scan;
But manly greatness men can span,
  And feel the bonds that draw.

THE SWAMP ANGEL[k]

There is a coal-black Angel
  With a thick Afric lip,
And he dwells (like the hunted and harried)
  In a swamp where the green frogs dip.
But his face is against a City
  Which is over a bay of the sea,
And he breathes with a breath that is blastment,
  And dooms by a far decree.

By night there is fear in the City,
  Through the darkness a star soareth on;
There's a scream that screams up to the zenith,
  Then the poise of a meteor lone—
Lighting far the pale fright of the faces,
  And downward the coming is seen;
Then the rush, and the burst, and the havoc,
  And wails and shrieks between.

It comes like the thief in the gloaming;
  It comes, and none may foretell
The place of the coming—the glaring;
  They live in a sleepless spell
That wizens, and withers, and whitens;
  It ages the young, and the bloom
Of the maiden is ashes of roses—
  The Swamp Angel broods in his gloom.

Swift is his messengers' going,
  But slowly he saps their halls,
As if by delay deluding.
  They move from their crumbling walls
Farther and farther away;
  But the Angel sends after and after,
By night with the flame of his ray—
  By night with the voice of his screaming—
Sends after them, stone by stone,
  And farther walls fall, farther portals,
And weed follows weed through the Town.

Is this the proud City? the scorner
  Which never would yield the ground?
Which mocked at the coal-black Angel?
  The cup of despair goes round.

Vainly she calls upon Michael
  (The white man's seraph was he),
For Michael has fled from his tower
  To the Angel over the sea.

Who weeps for the woeful City
  Let him weep for our guilty kind;
Who joys at her wild despairing—
  Christ, the Forgiver, convert his mind.

THE BATTLE FOR THE BAY
(August, 1864)

O mystery of noble hearts,
  To whom mysterious seas have been
In midnight watches, lonely calm and storm,
      A stern, sad discipline,
And rooted out the false and vain,
  And chastened them to aptness for
  Devotion and the deeds of war,
And death which smiles and cheers in spite of pain.

Beyond the bar the land-wind dies,
  The prow becharmed at anchor swim:
A summer night; the stars withdrawn look down—
      Fair eve of battle grim.
The sentries pace, bonetas glide;
  Below, the sleeping sailors swing,
  And in their dreams to quarters spring,
Or cheer their flag, or breast a stormy tide.

But drums are beat: *Up anchor all!*
  The triple lines steam slowly on;
Day breaks; along the sweep of decks each man
      Stands coldly by his gun—
As cold as it. But he shall warm—
  Warm with the solemn metal there,
  And all its ordered fury share,
In attitude a gladiatorial form.

The Admiral—yielding to the love
  Which held his life and ship so dear—
Sailed second in the long fleet's midmost line;
      Yet thwarted all their care:
He lashed himself aloft, and shone
  Star of the fight, with influence sent
  Throughout the dusk embattlement;
And so they neared the strait and walls of stone.

No sprightly fife as in the field,
  The decks were hushed like fanes in prayer;
Behind each man a holy angel stood—
      He stood, though none was 'ware.

Out spake the forts on either hand,
   Back speak the ships when spoken to,
   And set their flags in concert true,
And *On and in!* is Farragut's command.

But what delays? 'mid wounds above
   Dim buoys give hint of death below—
Sea-ambuscades, where evil art had aped
     Hecla that hides in snow.
The centre-van, entangled, trips;
   The starboard leader holds straight on:
   A cheer for the Tecumseh!—nay,
Before their eyes the turreted ship goes down!

The fire redoubles. While the fleet
   Hangs dubious—ere the horror ran—
The Admiral rushes to his rightful place—
     Well met! apt hour and man!—
Closes with peril, takes the lead,
His action is a stirring call;
He strikes his great heart through them all,
And is the genius of their daring deed.

The forts are daunted, slack their fire,
   Confounded by the deadlier aim
And rapid broadsides of the speeding fleet,
   And fierce denouncing flame.
Yet shots from four dark hulls embayed
   Come raking through the loyal crews,
   Whom now each dying mate endues
With his last look, anguished yet undismayed.

A flowering time to guilt is given,
   And traitors have their glorying hour;
A late, but sure, the righteous Paramount comes—
     Palsy is on their power!
So proved it with the rebel keels,
   The strong-holds past: assailed, they run;
   The Selma strikes, and the work is done:
The dropping anchor the achievement seals.

But no, she turns—the Tennessee!
   The solid Ram of iron and oak,

Strong as Evil, and bold as Wrong, though lone—
    A pestilence in her smoke.
The flagship is her singled mark,
    The wooden Hartford. Let her come;
    She challenges the planet of Doom,
And naught shall save her—not her iron bark.

Slip anchor, all! and at her, all!
    Bear down with rushing beaks—and now!
First the Monongahela struck—and reeled;
The Lackawana's prow
Next crashed—crashed, but not crashing; then
    The Admiral rammed, and rasping nigh
    Sloped in a broadside, which glanced by:
The Monitors battered at her adamant den.

The Chickasaw plunged beneath the stern
    And pounded there; a huge wrought orb
From the Manhattan pierced one wall, but dropped;
    Others the seas absorb.
Yet stormed on all sides, narrowed in,
    Hampered and cramped, the bad one fought—
    Spat ribald curses from the port
Whose shutters, jammed, locked up this Man-of-Sin.

No pause or stay. They made a din
    Like hammers round a boiler forged;
Now straining strength tangled itself with strength,
    Till Hate her will disgorged.
The white flag showed, the fight was won—
    Mad shouts went up that shook the Bay;
    But pale on the scarred fleet's decks there lay
A silent man for every silenced gun.

And quiet far below the wave,
    Where never cheers shall move their sleep,
Some who did boldly, nobly earn them, lie—
    Charmed children of the deep.
But decks that now are in the seed,
    And cannon yet within the mine,
    Shall thrill the deeper, gun and pine,
Because of the Tecumseh's glorious deed.

SHERIDAN AT CEDAR CREEK
(October, 1864)

Shoe the steed with silver
  That bore him to the fray,
When he heard the guns at dawning—
    Miles away;
When he heard them calling, calling—
  Mount! nor stay:
      Quick, or all is lost;
      They've surprised and stormed the post,
      They push your routed host—
Gallop! retrieve the day.

House the horse in ermine—
  For the foam-flake blew
White through the red October;
  He thundered into view;
They cheered him in the looming,
  Horseman and horse they knew.
      The turn of the tide began,
      The rally of bugles ran,
      He swung his hat in the van;
The electric hoof-spark flew.

Wreathe the steed and lead him—
  For the charge he led
Touched and turned the cypress
  Into amaranths for the head
Of Philip, king of riders,
  Who raised them from the dead.
      The camp (at dawning lost),
      By eve, recovered—forced,
      Rang with laughter of the host
At belated Early fled.

Shroud the horse in sable—
  For the mounds they heap!
There is firing in the Valley,
  And yet no strife they keep;

It is the parting volley,
  It is the pathos deep.
        There is glory for the brave
        Who lead, and nobly save,
        But no knowledge in the grave
Where the nameless followers sleep.

IN THE PRISON PEN
(1864)

Listless he eyes the palisades
  And sentries in the glare;
'Tis barren as a pelican-beach—
  But his world is ended there.

Nothing to do; and vacant hands
  Bring on the idiot-pain;
He tries to think—to recollect,
  But the blur is on his brain.

Around him swarm the plaining ghosts
  Like those on Virgil's shore—
A wilderness of faces dim,
  And pale ones gashed and hoar.

A smiting sun. No shed, no tree;
  He totters to his lair—
A den that sick hands dug in earth
  Ere famine wasted there,

Or, dropping in his place, he swoons,
  Walled in by throngs that press,
Till forth from the throngs they bear him dead—
  Dead in his meagreness.

THE COLLEGE COLONEL

He rides at their head;
  A crutch by his saddle just slants in view,
One slung arm is in splints, you see,
  Yet he guides his strong steed—how coldly too.

He brings his regiment home—
  Not as they filed two years before,
But a remnant half-tattered, and battered, and worn,
Like castaway sailors, who—stunned
    By the surf's loud roar,
  Their mates dragged back and seen no more—
Again and again breast the surge,
  And at last crawl, spent, to shore.

A still rigidity and pale—
  An Indian aloofness lones his brow;
He has lived a thousand years
Compressed in battle's pains and prayers,
  Marches and watches slow.
There are welcoming shouts, and flags;
  Old men off hat to the Boy,
Wreaths from gay balconies fall at his feet,
  But to *him*—there comes alloy.

It is not that a leg is lost,
  It is not that an arm is maimed,
It is not that the fever has racked—
  Self he has long disclaimed.

But all through the Seven Days' Fight,
  And deep in the Wilderness grim,
And in the field-hospital tent,
  And Petersburg crater, and dim
Lean brooding in Libby, there came—
  Ah heaven!—what *truth* to him.

THE EAGLE OF THE BLUE[1]

Aloft he guards the starry folds
    Who is the brother of the star;
The bird whose joy is in the wind
    Exulteth in the war.

No painted plume—a sober hue,
    His beauty is his power;
That eager calm of gaze intent
    Forsees the Sibyl's hour.

Austere, he crowns the swaying perch,
    Flapped by the angry flag;
The hurricane from the battery sings,
    But his claw has known the crag.

Amid the scream of shells, his scream
    Runs shrilling; and the glare
Of eyes that brave the blinding sun
    The volleyed flame can bear.

The pride of quenchless strength is his—
    Strength which, though chained, avails;
The very rebel looks and thrills—
    The anchored Emblem hails.

Though scarred in many a furious fray,
    No deadly hurt he knew;
Well may we think his years are charmed—
    The Eagle of the Blue.

A DIRGE FOR McPHERSON[m]
KILLED IN FRONT OF ATLANTA
(July, 1864)

Arms reversed and banners craped—
    Muffled drums;
Snowy horses sable-draped—
    McPherson comes.

> *But, tell us, shall we know him more,*
> *Lost-Mountain and lone Kenesaw?*

Brave the sword upon the pall—
    A gleam in gloom;
So a bright name lighteth all
    McPherson's doom.

Bear him through the chapel-door—
    Let priest in stole
Pace before the warrior
    Who led. Bell—toll!

Lay him down within the nave,
    The Lesson read—
Man is noble, man is brave,
    But man's—a weed.

Take him up again and wend
    Graveward, nor weep:
There's a trumpet that shall rend
    This Soldier's sleep.

Pass the ropes the coffin round,
    And let descend;
Prayer and volley—let it sound
    McPherson's end.

> *True fame is his, for life is o'er—*
> *Sarpedon of the mighty war.*

AT THE CANNON'S MOUTH
DESTRUCTION OF THE RAM ALBEMARLE BY THE TORPEDO-LAUNCH
(October, 1864)

Palely intent, he urged his keel
  Full on the guns, and touched the spring;
Himself involved in the bolt he drove
Timed with the armed hull's shot that stove
His shallop—die or do!
Into the flood his life he threw,
  Yet lives—unscathed—a breathing thing
To marvel at.

      He has his fame;
But that mad dash at death, how name?

Had Earth no charm to stay in the Boy
  The martyr-passion? Could he dare
Disdain the Paradise of opening joy
Which beckons the fresh heart every where?
Life has more lures than any girl
  For youth and strength; puts forth a share
Of beauty, hinting of yet rarer store;
And ever with unfathomable eyes,
    Which bafflingly entice,
Still strangely does Adonis draw.
And life once over, who shall tell the rest?
Life is, of all we know, God's best.
What imps these eagles then, that they
Fling disrespect on life by that proud way
In which they soar above our lower clay.

Pretence of wonderment and doubt unblest:
  In Cushing's eager deed was shown
  A spirit which brave poets own—
That scorn of life which earns life's crown;
  Earns, but not always wins; but *he*—
  The star ascended in his nativity.

THE MARCH TO THE SEA
(December, 1864)

Not Kenesaw high-arching,
  Nor Allatoona's glen—
Though there the graves lie parching—
  Stayed Sherman's miles of men;
From charred Atlanta marching
  They launched the sword again.
      The columns streamed like rivers
        Which in their course agree,
      And they streamed until their flashing
        Met the flashing of the sea:
          It was glorious glad marching,
          That marching to the sea.

They brushed the foe before them
  (Shall gnats impede the bull?);
Their own good bridges bore them
  Over swamps or torrents full,
And the grand pines waving o'er them
  Bowed to axes keen and cool.
      The columns grooved their channels,
        Enforced their own decree,
      And their power met nothing larger
        Until it met the sea:
          It was glorious glad marching,
          A marching glad and free.

Kilpatrick's snare of riders
  In zigzags mazed the land,
Perplexed the pale Southsiders
  With feints on every hand;
Vague menace awed the hiders
  In fort beyond command.
      To Sherman's shifting problem
        No foeman knew the key;
      But onward went the marching
        Unpausing to the sea:
          It was glorious glad marching,
          The swinging step was free.

The flankers ranged like pigeons
  In clouds through field or wood;
The flocks of all those regions,
  The herds and horses good,
Poured in and swelled the legions,
  For they caught the marching mood.
      A volley ahead! They hear it;
        And they hear the repartee:
      Fighting was but frolic
        In that marching to the sea:
          It was glorious glad marching,
          A marching bold and free.

All nature felt their coming,
  The birds like couriers flew,
And the banners brightly blooming
  The slaves by thousands drew,
And they marched beside the drumming,
  And they joined the armies blue.
      The cocks crowed from the cannon
        (Pets named from Grant and Lee),
      Plumed fighters and campaigners
        In that marching to the sea:
          It was glorious glad marching,
          For every man was free.

The foragers through calm lands
  Swept in tempest gay,
And they breathed the air of balm-lands
  Where rolled savannas lay,
And they helped themselves from farm-lands—
  As who should say them nay?
      The regiments uproarious
        Laughed in Plenty's glee;
      And they marched till their broad laughter
        Met the laughter of the sea:
          It was glorious glad marching,
          That marching to the sea.

The grain of endless acres
  Was threshed (as in the East)
By the trampling of the Takers,
  Strong march of man and beast;

The flails of those earth-shakers
 Left a famine where they ceased.
  The arsenals were yielded;
   The sword (that was to be),
   Arrested in the forging,
    Rued that marching to the sea:
     It was glorious glad marching,
     But ah, the stern decree!

For behind they left a wailing,
 A terror and a ban,
And blazing cinders sailing,
 And houseless households wan,
Wide zones of counties paling,
 And towns were maniacs ran,
   Was Treason's retribution?
   Necessity the plea?
   They will long remember Sherman
    And his streaming columns free—
     They will long remember Sherman
     Marching to the sea.

THE FRENZY IN THE WAKE[n]
SHERMAN'S ADVANCE THROUGH THE CAROLINAS
(February, 1865)

So strong to suffer, shall we be
 Weak to contend, and break
The sinews of the Oppressor's knee
 That grinds upon the neck?
   O, the garments rolled in blood
    Scorch in cities wrapped in flame,
   And the African—the imp!
   He gibbers, imputing shame.

Shall Time, avenging every woe,
 To us that joy allot
Which Israel thrilled when Sisera's brow
 Showed gaunt and showed the clot?

Curse on their foreheads, cheeks, and eyes—
  The Northern faces—true
To the flag we hate, the flag whose stars
  Like planets strike us through.

From frozen Maine they come,
  Far Minnesota too;
They come to a sun whose rays disown—
  May it wither them as the dew!
    The ghosts of our slain appeal:
      "Vain shall our victories be?"
    But back from its ebb the flood recoils—
      Back in a whelming sea.

With burning woods our skies are brass,
  The pillars of dust are seen;
The live-long day their cavalry pass—
  No crossing the road between.
      We were sore deceived—an awful host!
        They move like a roaring wind,
      Have we gamed and lost? but even despair
        Shall never our hate rescind.

THE FALL OF RICHMOND
THE TIDINGS RECEIVED IN THE NORTHERN METROPOLIS
(April, 1865)

What mean these peals from every tower,
  And crowds like seas that sway?
The cannon reply; they speak the heart
  Of the People impassioned, and say—
A city in flags for a city in flames,
  Richmond goes Babylon's way—
      Sing and pray.

O weary years and woeful wars,
  And armies in the grave;

But hearts unquelled at last deter
The helmed dilated Lucifer—
   Honor to Grant the brave,
Whose three stars now like Orion's rise
   When wreck is on the wave—
      Bless his glaive.

Well that the faith we firmly kept,
   And never our aim forswore
For the Terrors that trooped from each recess
When fainting we fought in the Wilderness,
   And Hell made loud hurrah;
But God is in Heaven, and Grant in the Town,
   And Right through might is Law—
      God's way adore.

THE SURRENDER AT APPOMATTOX
(April, 1865)

As billows upon billows roll,
   On victory victory breaks;
Ere yet seven days from Richmond's fall
   And crowning triumph wakes
The loud joy-gun, whose thunders run
   By sea-shore, streams, and lakes.
      The hope and great event agree
      In the sword that Grant received from Lee.

The warring eagles fold the wing,
   But not in Caesar's sway;
Not Rome o'ercome by Roman arms we sing
   As on Pharsalia's day,
But Treason thrown, though a giant grown,
   And Freedom's larger play.
      All human tribes glad token see
      In the close of the wars of Grant and Lee.

A CANTICLE:
SIGNIFICANT OF THE NATIONAL EXALTATION OF
ENTHUSIASM AT THE CLOSE OF THE WAR

O the precipice Titanic
  Of the congregated Fall,
And the angle oceanic
    Where the deepening thunders call—
      And the Gorge so grim,
      And the firmamental rim!
Multitudinously thronging
    The waters all converge,
Then they sweep adown in sloping
    Solidity of surge.

      The Nation, in her impulse
        Mysterious as the Tide,
      In emotion like an ocean
        Moves in power, not in pride;
      And is deep in her devotion
        As Humanity is wide.

      Thou Lord of hosts victorious,
        The confluence Thou hast twined;
      By a wondrous way and glorious
        A passage Thou dost find—
        A passage Thou dost find:
      Hosanna to the Lord of hosts,
        The hosts of human kind.

Stable in its baselessness
  When calm is in the air,
The Iris half in tracelessness
  Hovers faintly fair.
Fitfully assailing it
  A wind from heaven blows,
Shivering and paling it
  To blankness of the snows;
While, incessant in renewal,
  The Arch rekindled grows,
Till again the gem and jewel
  Whirl in blinding overthrows—

Till, prevailing and transcending,
  Lo, the Glory perfect there,
And the contest finds an ending,
  For repose is in the air.

But the foamy Deep unsounded,
  And the dim and dizzy ledge,
And the booming roar rebounded,
  And the gull that skims the edge!
    The Giant of the Pool
    Heaves his forehead white as wool—
Toward the Iris ever climbing
  From the Cataracts that call—
Irremovable vast arras
  Draping all the Wall.

      The Generations pouring
        From times of endless date,
      In their going, in their flowing
      Ever form the steadfast State;
        And Humanity is growing
        Toward the fullness of her fate.

      Thou Lord of hosts victorious,
        Fulfill the end designed;
      By a wondrous way and glorious
        A passage Thou dost find—
        A passage Thou dost find:
      Hosanna to the Lord of Hosts,
        The hosts of human kind.

THE MARTYR
INDICATIVE OF THE PASSION OF THE PEOPLE
ON THE 15TH DAY OF APRIL, 1865

Good Friday was the day
  Of the prodigy and crime,
When they killed him in his pity,
  When they killed him in his prime
Of clemency and calm—
    When with yearning he was filled
    To redeem the evil-willed,
And, though conqueror, be kind;
  But they killed him in his kindness,
  In their madness and their blindness,
And they killed him from behind.

    There is sobbing of the strong,
      And a pall upon the land;
    But the people in their weeping
      Bare the iron hand;
    Beware the People weeping
      When they bare the iron hand.

He lieth in his blood—
  The father in his face;
They have killed him, the Forgiver—
  The Avenger takes his place,"
The Avenger wisely stern,
    Who in righteousness shall do
    What the heavens call him to,
And the parricides remand;
  For they killed him in his kindness,
  In their madness and their blindness,
And his blood is on their hand.

    There is sobbing of the strong,
      And a pall upon the land;
    But the People in their weeping
      Bare the iron hand:
    Beware the People weeping
      When they bare the iron hand.

"THE COMING STORM":
A PICTURE BY S.R. GIFFORD, AND OWNED BY E. B.
INCLUDED IN THE N.A. EXHIBITION, APRIL 1865

All feeling hearts must feel for him
  Who felt this picture. Presage dim—
Dim inklings from the shadowy sphere
  Fixed him and fascinated here.

A demon-cloud like the mountain one
  Burst on a spirit as mild
As this urned lake, the home of shades,
  But Shakespeare's pensive child.

Never the lines had lightly scanned,
  Steeped in fable, steeped in fate;
The Hamlet in his heart was 'ware,
  Such hearts can antedate.

No utter surprise can come to him
  Who reaches Shakespeare's core;
That which we seek and shun is there—
  Man's final lore.

REBEL COLOR-BEARERS AT SHILOH[p]
A PLEA AGAINST THE VINDICTIVE CRY RAISED BY CIVILIANS
SHORTLY AFTER THE SURRENDER AT APPOMATTOX

The color-bearers facing death
White in the whirling sulphurous wreath,
  Stand boldly out before the line;
Right and left their glances go,
Proud of each other, glorying in their show;
Their battle-flags about them blow,
  And fold them as in flame divine:
Such living robes are only seen
Round martyrs burning on the green—
And martyrs for the Wrong have been.

Perish their Cause! but mark the men—
Mark the planted statues, then
Draw trigger on them if you can.

The leader of a patriot-band
Even so could view rebels who so could stand;
    And this when peril pressed him sore,
Left aidless in the shivered front of war—
    Skulkers behind, defiant foes before,
And fighting with a broken brand.
The challenge in that courage rare—
Courage defenseless, proudly bare—
Never could tempt him; he could dare
Strike up the leveled rifle there.

Sunday at Shiloh, and the day
When Stonewall charged—McClellan's crimson May,
And Chickamauga's wave of death,
And of the Wilderness the cypress wreath—
    All these have passed away.
The life in the veins of Treason lags,
Her daring color-bearers drop their flags,
    And yield. *Now* shall we fire?
            Can poor spite be?
Shall nobleness in victory less aspire
Than in reverse? Spare Spleen her ire,
    And think how Grant met Lee.

THE MUSTER[q]
SUGGESTED BY TWO DAYS REVIEW AT WASHINGTON
(May, 1865)

The Abrahamic river—
    Patriarch of floods,
Calls the roll of all his streams
    And watery multitudes:
        Torrent cries to torrent,
            The rapids hail the fall;
        With shouts the inland freshets
            Gather to the call.

The quotas of the Nation,
  Like the water-shed of waves,
Muster into union—
  Eastern warriors, Western braves.

Martial strains are mingling,
  Though distant far the bands,
And the wheeling of the squadrons
  Is like surf upon the sands.

The bladed guns are gleaming—
  Drift in lengthened trim,
Files on files for hazy miles—
  Nebulously dim.

O Milky Way of armies—
  Star rising after star,
New banners of the Commonwealths,
  And eagles of the War.

The Abrahamic river
  To sea-wide fullness fed,
Pouring from the thaw-lands
  By the God of floods is led:
    His deep enforcing current
      The streams of ocean own,
    And Europe's marge is evened
      By rills from Kansas lone.

AURORA-BOREALIS
COMMEMORATIVE OF THE DISSOLUTION OF ARMIES AT THE PEACE
(May, 1865)

What power disbands the Northern Lights
  After their steely play?
The lonely watcher feels an awe
  Of Nature's sway,
    As when appearing,
    He marked their flashed uprearing
In the cold gloom—

Retreatings and advancings,
(Like dallyings of doom),
Transitions and enhancings,
And bloody ray.

The phantom-host has failed quite,
Splendor and Terror gone—
Portent or promise—and gives way
To pale, meek Dawn;
The coming, going,
Alike in wonder showing—
Alike the God,
Decreeing and commanding
The million blades that glowed,
The muster and disbanding—
Midnight and Morn.

THE RELEASED REBEL PRISONER[r]
(June, 1865)

Armies he's seen—the herds of war,
But never such swarms of men
As now in the Nineveh of the North—
How mad the Rebellion then!

And yet but dimly he divines
The depth of that deceit,
And superstition of vast pride
Humbled to such defeat.

Seductive shone the Chiefs in arms—
His steel the nearest magnet drew;
Wreathed with its kind, the Gulf-weed drives—
'Tis Nature's wrong they rue.

His face is hidden in his beard,
But his heart peers out at eye—
And such a heart! like a mountain-pool
Where no man passes by.

He thinks of Hill—a brave soul gone;
  And Ashby dead in pale disdain;
And Stuart with the Rupert-plume,
  Whose blue eye never shall laugh again.

He hears the drum; he sees our boys
  From his wasted fields return;
Ladies feast them on strawberries,
  And even to kiss them yearn.

He marks them bronzed, in soldier-trim,
  The rifle proudly borne;
They bear it for an heir-loom home,
  And he—disarmed—jail-worn.

Home, home—his heart is full of it:
  But home he never shall see,
Even should he stand upon the spot;
  'Tis gone!—where his brothers be.

The cypress-moss from tree to tree
  Hangs in his Southern land;
As drear, from thought to thought of his
  Run memories hand in hand.

And so he lingers—lingers on
  In the City of the Foe—
His cousins and his countrymen
  Who see him listless go.

A GRAVE NEAR PETERSBURG, VIRGINIA[s]

Head-board and foot-board duly placed—
  Grassed is the mound between;
Daniel Drouth is the slumberer's name—
  Long may his grave be green!

Quick was his way—a flash and a blow,
  Full of his fire was he—
A fire of hell—'tis burnt out now—
  Green may his grave long be!

May his grave be green, though he
  Was a rebel of iron mould:
Many a true heart—true to the Cause,
  Though the blaze of his wrath lies cold.

May his grave be green—still green
  While happy years shall run;
May none come nigh to disinter
  The—*Buried Gun.*

"FORMERLY A SLAVE"
AN IDEALIZED PORTRAIT, BY E. VEDDER, IN THE SPRING
EXHIBITION OF THE NATIONAL ACADEMY, 1865

The sufferance of her race is shown,
  And retrospect of life,
Which now too late deliverance dawns upon;
  Yet is she not at strife.

Her children's children they shall know
  The good withheld from her;
And so her reverie takes prophetic cheer—
  In spirit she sees the stir

Far down the depth of thousand years,
  And marks the revel shine;
Her dusky face is lit with sober light,
  Sibylline, yet benign.

THE APPARITION
(A RETROSPECT.)

Convulsions came; and, where the field
  Long slept in pastoral green,
A goblin-mountain was upheaved
(Sure the scared sense was all deceived),
  Marl-glen and slag-ravine.

The unreserve of Ill was there,
　　The clinkers in her last retreat;
But, ere the eye could take it in,
Or mind could comprehension win,
　　It sunk!—and at our feet.

So, then, Solidity's a crust—
　　The core of fire below;
All may go well for many a year,
But who can think without a fear
　　Of horrors that happen so?

MAGNANIMITY BAFFLED

"Sharp words we had before the fight;
　　But—now the fight is done—
Look, here's my hand," said the Victor bold,
　　"Take it—an honest one!
What, holding back? I mean you well;
　　Though worsted, you strove stoutly, man;
The odds were great; I honor you;
　　Man honors man.

"Still silent, friend? can grudges be?
　　Yet am I held a foe?—
Turned to the wall, on his cot he lies—
　　Never I'll leave him so!
Brave one! I here implore your hand;
　　Dumb still? all fellowship fled?
Nay, then, I'll have this stubborn hand!"
　　He snatched it—it was dead.

ON THE SLAIN COLLEGIANS[t]

Youth is the time when hearts are large,
　　And stirring wars
Appeal to the spirit which appeals in turn
　　To the blade it draws.

If woman incite, and duty show
  (Though made the mask of Cain),
Or whether it be Truth's sacred cause,
    Who can aloof remain
That shares youth's ardor, uncooled by the snow
    Of wisdom or sordid gain?

The liberal arts and nurture sweet
Which give his gentleness to man—
  Train him to honor, lend him grace
Through bright examples meet—
That culture which makes never wan
With underminings deep, but holds
  The surface still, its fitting place,
  And so gives sunniness to the face
And bravery to the heart; what troops
  Of generous boys in happiness thus bred—
  Saturnians through life's Tempe led,
Went from the North and came from the South,
With golden mottoes in the mouth,
  To lie down midway on a bloody bed.

Woe for the homes of the North,
And woe for the seats of the South:
All who felt life's spring in prime,
And were swept by the wind of their place and time—
  All lavish hearts, on whichever side,
Of birth urbane or courage high,
Armed them for the stirring wars—
Armed them—some to die.
        Apollo-like in pride,
Each would slay his Python—caught
The maxims in his temple taught—
  Aflame with sympathies whose blaze
Perforce enwrapped him—social laws,
  Friendship and kin, and by-gone days—
Vows, kisses—every heart unmoors,
And launches into the seas of wars.
What could they else—North or South?
Each went forth with blessings given
By priests and mothers in the name of Heaven;
        And honor in all was chief.

Warred one for Right, and one for Wrong?
So put it; but they both were young—
Each grape to his cluster clung,
All their elegies are sung.

The anguish of maternal hearts
    Must search for balm divine;
But well the striplings bore their fated parts
    (The heavens all parts assign)—
Never felt life's care or cloy.
Each bloomed and died an unabated Boy;
Nor dreamed what death was—thought it mere
Sliding into some vernal sphere.
They knew the joy, but leaped the grief,
Like plants that flower ere comes the leaf—
Which storms lay low in kindly doom,
And kill them in their flush of bloom.

AMERICA

I

Where the wings of a sunny Dome expand
I saw a Banner in gladsome air—
Starry, like Berenice's Hair—
Afloat in broadened bravery there;
With undulating long-drawn flow,
As rolled Brazilian billows go
Voluminously o'er the Line.
The Land reposed in peace below;
    The children in their glee
Were folded to the exulting heart
    Of young Maternity.

II

Later, and it streamed in fight
    When tempest mingled with the fray,

And over the spear-point of the shaft
  I saw the ambiguous lightning play.
Valor with Valor strove, and died:
Fierce was Despair, and cruel was Pride;
And the lorn Mother speechless stood,
Pale at the fury of her brood.

III

Yet later, and the silk did wind
    Her fair cold form;
Little availed the shining shroud,
  Though ruddy in hue, to cheer or warm,
A watcher looked upon her low, and said—
She sleeps, but sleeps, she is not dead.
  But in that sleep contortion showed
The terror of the vision there—
  A silent vision unavowed,
Revealing earth's foundation bare,
  And Gorgon in her hidden place.
It was a thing of fear to see
  So foul a dream upon so fair a face,
And the dreamer lying in that starry shroud.

IV

But from the trance she sudden broke—
  The trance, or death into promoted life;
At her feet a shivered yoke,
And in her aspect turned to heaven
  No trace of passion or of strife—
A clear calm look. It spake of pain,
But such as purifies from stain—
Sharp pangs that never come again—
  And triumph repressed by knowledge meet,
Power dedicate, and hope grown wise,
  And youth matured for age's seat—
Law on her brow and empire in her eyes.
  So she, with graver air and lifted flag;
While the shadow, chased by light,
Fled along the far-drawn height,
  And left her on the crag.

ON THE HOME GUARDS
WHO PERISHED IN THE DEFENSE OF LEXINGTON, MISSOURI

The men who here in harness died
  Fell not in vain, though in defeat.
They by their end well fortified
  The Cause, and built retreat
(With memory of their valor tried)
For emulous in many an after fray—
Hearts sore beset, which died at bay.

INSCRIPTION
FOR THE GRAVES AT PEA RIDGE, ARKANSAS

Let none misgive we died amiss
  When here we strove in furious fight:
Furious it was; nathless was this
  Better than tranquil plight,
And tame surrender of the Cause
Hallowed by hearts and by the laws.
  We here who warred for Man and Right,
The choice of warring never laid with us.
  There we were ruled by the traitor's choice.
  Nor long we stood to trim and poise,
But marched, and fell—victorious!

THE FORTITUDE OF THE NORTH
UNDER THE DISASTER OF THE SECOND MANASSAS

No shame they take for dark defeat
  While prizing yet each victory won,
Who fight for the Right through all retreat,
  Nor pause until their work is done.

The Cape-of-Storms is proof to every throe;
   Vainly against that foreland beat
Wild winds aloft and wilder waves below:
The black cliffs gleam through rents in sleet
When the livid Antarctic storm-clouds glow.

ON THE MEN OF MAINE
KILLED IN THE VICTORY OF BATON ROUGE, LOUISIANA

Afar they fell. It was the zone
   Of fig and orange, cane and lime
(A land how all unlike their own,
With the cold pine-grove overgrown),
   But still their Country's clime.
And there in youth they died for her—
      The Volunteers,
For her went up their dying prayers:
   So vast the Nation, yet so strong the tie.
What doubt shall come, then, to deter
   The Republic's earnest faith and courage high.

AN EPITAPH

When Sunday tidings from the front
   Made pale the priest and people,
And heavily the blessing went,
   And bells were dumb in the steeple;
The Soldier's widow (summering sweetly here,
   In shade by waving beeches lent)
   Felt deep at heart her faith content,
And priest and people borrowed of her cheer.

INSCRIPTION
FOR MARYE'S HEIGHTS, FREDERICKSBURG

To them who crossed the flood
And climbed the hill, with eyes
   Upon the heavenly flag intent,
   And through the deathful tumult went
Even unto death: to them this Stone—
Erect, where they were overthrown—
   Of more than victory the monument.

THE MOUND BY THE LAKE

The grass shall never forget this grave.
When homeward footing it in the sun
   After the weary ride by rail,
The stripling soldiers passed her door,
   Wounded perchance, or wan and pale,
She left her household work undone—
Duly the wayside table spread,
   With evergreens shaded, to regale
Each travel-spent and grateful one.
So warm her heart—childless—unwed,
Who like a mother comforted.

ON THE SLAIN AT CHICKAMAUGA

Happy are they and charmed in life
   Who through long wars arrive unscarred
At peace. To such the wreath be given,
If they unfalteringly have striven—
   In honor, as in limb, unmarred.
Let cheerful praise be rife,
   And let them live their years at ease,
Musing on brothers who victorious died—
   Loved mates whose memory shall ever please.

And yet mischance is honorable too—
　　Seeming defeat in conflict justified
Whose end to closing eyes is hid from view.
The will, that never can relent—
The aim, survivor of the bafflement,
　　Make this memorial due.

AN UNINSCRIBED MONUMENT
ON ONE OF THE BATTLE-FIELDS OF THE WILDERNESS

Silence and Solitude may hint
　　(Whose home is in yon piny wood)
What I, though tableted, could never tell—
The din which here befell,
　　And striving of the multitude.
The iron cones and spheres of death
　　Set round me in their rust,
　　　　These, too, if just,
Shall speak with more than animated breath.
　　Thou who beholdest, if thy thought,
Not narrowed down to personal cheer,
Take in the import of the quiet here—
　　The after-quiet—the calm full fraught;
Thou too wilt silent stand—
Silent as I, and lonesome as the land.

ON SHERMAN'S MEN
WHO FELL IN THE ASSAULT OF KENESAW MOUNTAIN, GEORGIA

They said that Fame her clarion dropped
　　Because great deeds were done no more—
That even Duty knew no shining ends,
And Glory—'twas a fallen star!
　　But battle can heroes and bards restore.
　　　　Nay, look at Kenesaw:
Perils the mailed ones never knew
Are lightly braved by the ragged coats of blue,
And gentler hearts are bared to deadlier war.

ON THE GRAVE OF A YOUNG CAVALRY OFFICER KILLED IN THE VALLEY OF VIRGINIA

Beauty and youth, with manners sweet, and friends—
   Gold, yet a mind not unenriched had he
Whom here low violets veil from eyes.
   But all these gifts transcended be:
His happier fortune in this mound you see.

A REQUIEM
FOR SOLDIERS LOST IN OCEAN TRANSPORTS

When, after storms that woodlands rue,
   To valleys comes atoning dawn,
The robins blithe their orchard-sports renew;
   And meadow-larks, no more withdrawn,
Caroling fly in the languid blue;
The while, from many a hid recess,
Alert to partake the blessedness,
The pouring mites their airy dance pursue.
   So, after ocean's ghastly gales,
When laughing light of hoyden morning breaks,
      Every finny hider wakes—
From vaults profound swims up with glittering scales;
   Through the delightsome sea he sails,
With shoals of shining tiny things
Frolic on every wave that flings
   Against the prow its showery spray;
All creatures joying in the morn,
Save them forever from joyance torn,
   Whose bark was lost where now the dolphins play;
Save them that by the fabled shore,
   Down the pale stream are washed away,
Far to the reef of bones are borne;
   And never revisits them the light,
Nor sight of long-sought land and pilot more;
   Nor heed they now the lone bird's flight
Round the lone spar where mid-sea surges pour.

ON A NATURAL MONUMENT
IN A FIELD OF GEORGIA

No trophy this—a Stone unhewn,
  And stands where here the field immures
The nameless brave whose palms are won.
Outcast they sleep; yet fame is nigh—
  Pure fame of deeds, not doers;
Nor deeds of men who bleeding die
  In cheer of hymns that round them float:
In happy dreams such close the eye.
But withering famine slowly wore,
  And slowly fell disease did gloat.
Even Nature's self did aid deny;
In horror they choked the pensive sigh.
  Yea, off from home sad Memory bore
(Though anguished Yearning heaved that way),
Lest wreck of reason might befall.
  As men in gales shun the lee shore,
Though there the homestead be, and call,
And thitherward winds and waters sway—
As such lorn mariners, so fared they.
But naught shall now their peace molest.
  Their fame is this: they did endure—
Endure, when fortitude was vain
To kindle any approving strain
Which they might hear. To these who rest,
  This healing sleep alone was sure.

COMMEMORATIVE OF A NAVAL VICTOR

Sailors there are of gentlest breed,
  Yet strong, like every goodly thing;
The discipline of arms refines,
  And the wave gives tempering.
  The damasked blade its beam can fling;
It lends the last grave grace:

The hawk, the hound, and sworded nobleman
  In Titian's picture for a king,
Are of hunter or warrior race.

In social halls a favored guest
  In years that follow victory won,
How sweet to feel your festal fame
  In woman's glance instinctive thrown:
  Repose is yours—your deed is known,
It musks the amber wine;
It lives, and sheds a light from storied days
  Rich as October sunsets brown,
Which make the barren place to shine.

But seldom the laurel wreath is seen
  Unmixed with pensive pansies dark;
There's a light and a shadow on every man
  Who at last attains his lifted mark—
  Nursing through night the ethereal spark.
Elate he never can be;
He feels that spirit which glad had hailed his worth,
  Sleep in oblivion.—The shark
Glides white through the phosphorus sea.

PRESENTATION TO THE AUTHORITIES
BY PRIVATES, OF COLORS CAPTURED IN BATTLES ENDING
IN THE SURRENDER OF LEE

These flags of armies overthrown—
Flags fallen beneath the sovereign one
In end foredoomed which closes war;
We here, the captors, lay before
  The altar which of right claims all—
Our Country. And as freely we,
  Revering ever her sacred call,
Could lay our lives down—though life be
Thrice loved and precious to the sense
Of such as reap the recompense
  Of life imperiled for just cause—

Imperiled, and yet preserved;
While comrades, whom Duty as strongly nerved,
Whose wives were all as dear, lie low.
But these flags given, glad we go
   To waiting homes with vindicated laws.

THE RETURNED VOLUNTEER TO HIS RIFLE

Over this hearth—my father's seat—
   Repose, to patriot-memory dear,
Thou tried companion, whom at last I greet
   By steepy banks of Hudson here.
How oft I told thee of this scene—
The Highlands blue—the river's narrowing sheen.
Little at Gettysburg we thought
To find such haven; but God kept it green.
Long rest! with belt, and bayonet, and canteen.

THE SCOUT TOWARD ALDIE.

The cavalry-camp lies on the slope
  Of what was late a vernal hill,
But now like a pavement bare—
An outpost in the perilous wilds
  Which ever are lone and still;
      But Mosby's men are there—
      Of Mosby best beware.

Great trees the troopers felled, and leaned
  In antlered walls about their tents;
Strict watch they kept; 'twas *Hark!* and *Mark!*
Unarmed none cared to stir abroad
  For berries beyond their forest-fence:
      As glides in seas the shark,
      Rides Mosby through green dark.

All spake of him, but few had seen
  Except the maimed ones or the low;
Yet rumor made him every thing—
A farmer—woodman—refugee—
  The man who crossed the field but now;
      A spell about his life did cling—
      Who to the ground shall Mosby bring?

The morning-bugles lonely play,
  Lonely the evening-bugle calls—
Unanswered voices in the wild;
The settled hush of birds in nest
  Becharms, and all the wood enthralls:
      Memory's self is so beguiled
      That Mosby seems a satyr's child.

They lived as in the Eerie Land—
  The fire-flies showed with fairy gleam;
And yet from pine-tops one might ken
The Capitol Dome—hazy—sublime—
  A vision breaking on a dream:
      So strange it was that Mosby's men
      Should dare to prowl where the Dome was seen.

A ride toward Aldie broke the spell.—
  The Leader lies before his tent
Gazing at heaven's all-cheering lamp
Through blandness of a morning rare;
    His thoughts on bitter-sweets are bent:
      His sunny bride is in the camp—
      But Mosby—graves are beds of damp!

The trumpet calls; he goes within;
  But none the prayer and sob may know:
Her hero he, but bridegroom too.
Ah, love in a tent is a queenly thing,
  And fame, be sure, refines the vow;
      But fame fond wives have lived to rue,
      And Mosby's men fell deeds can do.

Tan-tara! tan-tara! tan-tara!
  Mounted and armed he sits a king;
For pride she smiles if now she peep—
Elate he rides at the head of his men;
  He is young, and command is a boyish thing:
      They file out into the forest deep—
      Do Mosby and his rangers sleep?

The sun is gold, and the world is green,
  Opal the vapors of morning roll;
The champing horses lightly prance—
Full of caprice, and the riders too
  Curving in many a caricole.
      But marshaled soon, by fours advance—
      Mosby had checked that airy dance.

By the hospital-tent the cripples stand—
  Bandage, and crutch, and cane, and sling,
And palely eye the brave array;
The froth of the cup is gone for them
  (Caw! caw! the crows through the blueness wing):
      Yet these were late as bold, as gay;
      But Mosby—a clip, and grass is hay.

How strong they feel on their horses free,
  Tingles the tendoned thigh with life;
Their cavalry jackets make boys of all—

With golden breasts like the oriole;
  The chat, the jest, and laugh are rife.
      But word is passed from the front—a call
      For order; the wood is Mosby's hall.

To which behest one rider sly
  (Spurred, but unarmed) gave little heed—
Of dexterous fun not slow or spare,
He teased his neighbors of touchy mood,
  Into plungings he pricked his steed:
      A black-eyed man on a coal-black mare,
      Alive as Mosby in mountain air.

His limbs were long, and large, and round;
  He whispered, winked—did all but shout:
A healthy man for the sick to view;
The taste in his mouth was sweet at morn;
  Little of care he cared about.
      And yet of pains and pangs he knew—
      In others, maimed by Mosby's crew.

The Hospital Steward—even he
  (Sacred in person as a priest),
And on his coat-sleeve broidered nice
Wore the caduceus, black and green.
  No wonder he sat so light on his beast;
      This cheery man in suit of price
      Not even Mosby dared to slice.

They pass the picket by the pine
  And hollow log—a lonesome place;
His horse adroop, and pistol clean;
'Tis cocked—kept leveled toward the wood;
  Strained vigilance ages his childish face.
      Since midnight has that stripling been
      Peering for Mosby through the green.

Splashing they cross the freshet-flood,
  And up the muddy bank they strain;
A horse at a spectral white-ash shies—
One of the span of the ambulance,
  Black as a hearse. They give the rein:

    Silent speed on a scout were wise,
    Could cunning baffle Mosby's spies.

Rumor had come that a band was lodged
    In green retreats of hills that peer
By Aldie (famed for the swordless charge᭄).
Much store they'd heaped of captured arms
    And, peradventure, pilfered cheer;
        For Mosby's lads oft hearts enlarge
        In revelry by some gorge's marge.

"Don't let your sabres rattle and ring;
    To his oat-bag let each man give heed—
There now, that fellow's bag's untied,
Sowing the road with the precious grain.
    Your carbines swing at hand—you need!
        Look to yourselves, and your nags beside,
        Men who after Mosby ride."

Picked lads and keen went sharp before—
    A guard, though scarce against surprise;
And rearmost rode an answering troop,
But flankers none to right or left.
    No bugle peals, no pennon flies:
        Silent they sweep, and fain would swoop
        On Mosby with an Indian whoop.

On, right on through the forest land,
    Nor man, nor maid, nor child was seen—
Not even a dog. The air was still;
The blackened hut they turned to see,
    And spied charred benches on the green;
        A squirrel sprang from the rotting mill
        Whence Mosby sallied late, brave blood to spill.

By worn-out fields they cantered on—
    Drear fields amid the woodlands wide;
By cross-roads of some olden time,
In which grew groves; by gate-stones down—
    Grassed ruins of secluded pride:
        A strange lone land, long past the prime,
        Fit land for Mosby or for crime.

The brook in the dell they pass. One peers
  Between the leaves: "Ay, there's the place—
There, on the oozy ledge—'twas there
We found the body (Blake's, you know);
  Such whirlings, gurglings round the face—
      Shot drinking! Well, in war all's fair—
      So Mosby says. The bough—take care!"

Hard by, a chapel. Flower-pot mould
  Danked and decayed the shaded roof;
The porch was punk; the clapboards spanned
With ruffled lichens gray or green;
  Red coral-moss was not aloof;
      And mid dry leaves green dead-man's-hand
      Groped toward that chapel in Mosby-land.

They leave the road and take the wood,
  And mark the trace of ridges there—
A wood where once had slept the farm—
A wood where once tobacco grew
  Drowsily in the hazy air,
      And wrought in all kind things a calm—
      Such influence, Mosby! bids disarm.

To ease even yet the place did woo—
  To ease which pines unstirring share,
For ease the weary horses sighed:
Halting, and slackening girths, they feed,
  Their pipes they light, they loiter there;
      Then up, and urging still the Guide,
      On, and after Mosby ride.

This Guide in frowzy coat of brown,
  And beard of ancient growth and mould,
Bestrode a bony steed and strong,
As suited well with bulk he bore—
  A wheezy man with depth of hold
      Who jouncing went. A staff he swung—
      A wight whom Mosby's wasp had stung.

Burnt out and homeless—hunted long!
  That wheeze he caught in autumn-wood
Crouching (a fat man) for his life,

And spied his lean son 'mong the crew
  That probed the covert. Ah! black blood
     Was his 'gainst even child and wife—
     Fast friends to Mosby. Such the strife.

A lad, unhorsed by sliding girths,
  Strains hard to readjust his seat
Ere the main body show the gap
'Twixt them and the rear-guard; scrub-oaks near
  He sidelong eyes, while hands move fleet;
     Then mounts and spurs. One drops his cap—
     "Let Mosby find!" nor heeds mishap.

A gable time-stained peeps through trees:
"You mind the fight in the haunted house?
That's it; we clenched them in the room—
An ambuscade of ghosts we thought,
  But proved sly rebels on a bouse!
     Luke lies in the yard." The chimneys loom:
     Some muse on Mosby—some on doom.

Less nimbly now through brakes they wind,
  And ford wild creeks where men have drowned;
The pool they skirt, avoid the fen,
And so till night, when down they lie,
  Their steeds still saddled, in wooded ground:
     Rein in hand they slumber then,
     Dreaming of Mosby's cedarn den.

But Colonel and Major friendly sat
  Where boughs deformed low made a seat.
The Young Man talked (all sworded and spurred)
Of the partisan's blade he longed to win,
  And frays in which he meant to beat.
     The grizzled Major smoked, and heard:
     "But what's that—Mosby?" "No, a bird."

A contrast here like sire and son,
  Hope and Experience sage did meet;
The Youth was brave, the Senior too;
But through the Seven Days one had served,
  And gasped with the rear-guard in retreat:
     So he smoked and smoked, and the wreath he blew—
     "Any *sure* news of Mosby's crew?"

He smoked and smoked, eyeing the while
  A huge tree hydra-like in growth—
Moon-tinged—with crook'd boughs rent or lopped—
Itself a haggard forest. "Come!"
    The Colonel cried, "to talk you're loath;
      D'ye hear? I say he must be stopped,
      This Mosby—caged, and hair close cropped."

"Of course; but what's that dangling there?"
  "Where?" "From the tree—that gallows-bough;"
"A bit of frayed bark, is it not?"
"Ay—or a rope; did *we* hang last?—
  Don't like my neckerchief any how;"
    He loosened it: "O ay, we'll stop
    This Mosby—but that vile jerk and drop!"ᵂ

By peep of light they feed and ride,
  Gaining a grove's green edge at morn,
And mark the Aldie hills uprear
And five gigantic horsemen carved
  Clear-cut against the sky withdrawn;
    Are more behind? an open snare?
    Or Mosby's men but watchmen there?

The ravaged land was miles behind,
  And Loudon spread her landscape rare;
Orchards in pleasant lowlands stood,
Cows were feeding, a cock loud crew,
  But not a friend at need was there;
    The valley-folk were only good
    To Mosby and his wandering brood.

What best to do? what mean yon men?
  Colonel and Guide their minds compare;
Be sure some looked their Leader through;
Dismounted, on his sword he leaned
  As one who feigns an easy air;
    And yet perplexed he was they knew—
    Perplexed by Mosby's mountain-crew.

The Major hemmed as he would speak,
  But checked himself, and left the ring

Of cavalrymen about their Chief—
Young courtiers mute who paid their court
  By looking with confidence on their king;
      They knew him brave, foresaw no grief—
      But Mosby—the time to think is brief.

The Surgeon (sashed in sacred green)
  Was glad 'twas not for *him* to say
What next should be; if a trooper bleeds,
Why he will do his best, as wont,
  And his partner in black will aid and pray;
      But judgment bides with him who leads,
      And Mosby many a problem breeds.

This Surgeon was the kindliest man
  That ever a callous trade professed;
He felt for him, that Leader young,
And offered medicine from his flask:
  The Colonel took it with marvelous zest.
      For such fine medicine good and strong,
      Oft Mosby and his foresters long.

A charm of proof. "Ho, Major, come—
  Pounce on yon men! Take half your troop,
Through the thickets wind—pray speedy be—
And gain their rear. And, Captain Morn,
  Picket these roads—all travelers stop;
      The rest to the edge of this crest with me,
      That Mosby and his scouts may see."

Commanded and done. Ere the sun stood steep,
  Back came the Blues, with a troop of Grays,
Ten riding double—luckless ten!—
Five horses gone, and looped hats lost,
  And love-locks dancing in a maze—
      Certes, but sophomores from the glen
      Of Mosby—not his veteran men.

"Colonel," said the Major, touching his cap,
  "We've had our ride, and here they are."
"Well done! how many found you there?"
"As many as I bring you here."

"And no one hurt?" "There'll be no scar—
　　One fool was battered." "Find their lair?"
　　"Why, Mosby's brood camp every where."

He sighed, and slid down from his horse,
　And limping went to a spring-head nigh.
"Why, bless me, Major, not hurt, I hope?"
"Battered my knee against a bar
　When the rush was made; all right by-and-by.—
　　　Halloa! they gave you too much rope—
　　　Go back to Mosby, eh? elope?"

Just by the low-hanging skirt of wood
　The guard, remiss, had given a chance
For a sudden sally into the cover—
But foiled the intent, nor fired a shot,
　Though the issue was a deadly trance;
　　　For, hurled 'gainst an oak that humped low over,
　　　Mosby's man fell, pale as a lover.

They pulled some grass his head to ease
　(Lined with blue shreds a ground-nest stirred).
The Surgeon came—"Here's a to-do!"
"Ah!" cried the Major, darting a glance,
　"This fellow's the one that fired and spurred
　　　Down hill, but met reserves below—
　　　My boys, not Mosby's—so we go!"

The Surgeon—bluff, red, goodly man—
　Kneeled by the hurt one; like a bee
He toiled. The pale young Chaplain too—
(Who went to the wars for cure of souls,
　And his own student-ailments)—he
　　　Bent over likewise; spite the two
　　　Mosby's poor man more pallid grew.

Meanwhile the mounted captives near
　Jested; and yet they anxious showed;
Virginians; some of family-pride,
And young, and full of fire, and fine
　In open feature and cheek that glowed;
　　　And here thralled vagabonds now they ride—
　　　but list! one speaks for Mosby's side.

"Why, three to one—your horses strong—
  Revolvers, rifles, and a surprise—
Surrender we account no shame!
We live, are gay, and life is hope;
  We'll fight again when fight is wise.
      There are plenty more from where we came;
      But go find Mosby—start the game!"

Yet one there was who looked but glum;
  In middle-age, a father he,
And this his first experience too:
"They shot at my heart when my hands were up—
  This fighting's crazy work, I see!"
      But noon is high; what next to do?
      The woods are mute, and Mosby is the foe.

"Save what we've got," the Major said;
  "Bad plan to make a scout too long;
The tide may turn, and drag them back,
And more beside. These rides I've been,
  And every time a mine was sprung.
      To rescue, mind, they won't be slack—
      Look out for Mosby's rifle-crack."

"We welcome it! give crack for crack!
  Peril, old lad, is what I seek."
"O then, there's plenty to be had—
By all means on, and have our fill!"
  With that, grotesque, he writhed his neck,
      Showing a scar by buck-shot made—
      Kind Mosby's Christmas gift, he said.

"But, Colonel, my prisoners—let a guard
  Make sure of them, and lead to camp.
That done, we're free for a dark-room fight
If so you say." The other laughed;
  "Trust me, Major, nor throw a damp.
      But first to try a little sleight—
      Sure news of Mosby would suit me quite."

Herewith he turned—"Reb, have a dram?"
  Holding the Surgeon's flask with a smile
To a young scapegrace from the glen.

"Oh yes!" he eagerly replied,
  "And thank you, Colonel, but—any guile?
    For if you think we'll blab—why, then
    You don't know Mosby or his men."

The Leader's genial air relaxed.
  "Best give it up," a whisperer said.
"By heaven, I'll range their rebel den!"
"They'll treat you well," the captive cried;
  "They're all like us—handsome—well-bred;
    In wood or town, with sword or pen,
    Polite is Mosby, bland his men."

"Where were you, lads, last night?—come, tell!"
  "We?—at a wedding in the Vale—
The bridegroom our comrade; by his side
Belisent, my cousin—O, so proud
  Of her young love with old wounds pale—
    A Virginian girl! God bless her pride—
    Of a crippled Mosby-man the bride!"

"Four walls shall mend that saucy mood,
  And moping prisons tame him down,"
Said Captain Cloud. "God help that day,"
Cried Captain Morn, "and he so young.
  But hark, he sings—a madcap one!"
    "O, we multiply merrily in the May,
    The birds and Mosby's men, they say!"

While echoes ran, a wagon old,
  Under stout guard of Corporal Chew
Came up; a lame horse, dingy white,
With clouted harness; ropes in hand,
  Cringed the humped driver, black in hue;
    By him (for Mosby's band a sight)
    A sister-rebel sat, her veil held tight.

"I picked them up," the Corporal said,
  "Crunching their way over stick and root,
Through yonder wood. The man here—Cuff—
Says they are going to Leesburg town."
  The Colonel's eye took in the group;
    The veiled one's hand he spied—enough!
    Not Mosby's. Spite the gown's poor stuff,

Off went his hat: "Lady, fear not;
  We soldiers do what we deplore—
I must detain you till we march."
The stranger nodded. Nettled now,
  He grew politer than before:—
      "'Tis Mosby's fault, this halt and search:"
      The lady stiffened in her starch.

"My duty, madam, bids me now
  Ask what may seem a little rude.
Pardon—that veil—withdraw it, please
(Corporal! make every man fall back);
  Pray, now, I do but what I should;
      Bethink you, 'tis in masks like these
      That Mosby haunts the villages."

Slowly the stranger drew her veil,
  And looked the Soldier in the eye—
A glance of mingled foul and fair;
Sad patience in a proud disdain,
  And more than quietude. A sigh
      She heaved, as if all unaware,
      And far seemed Mosby from her care.

She came from Yewton Place, her home,
  So ravaged by the war's wild play—
Campings, and foragings, and fires—
That now she sought an aunt's abode.
  Her kinsmen? In Lee's army, they.
      The black? A servant, late her sire's.
      And Mosby? Vainly he inquires.

He gazed, and sad she met his eye;
  "In the wood yonder were you lost?"
No; at the forks they left the road
Because of hoof-prints (thick they were—
  Thick as the words in notes thrice crossed),
      And fearful, made that episode.
      In fear of Mosby? None she showed.

Her poor attire again he scanned:
  "Lady, once more; I grieve to jar
On all sweet usage, but must plead
To have what peeps there from your dress;

That letter—'tis justly prize of war."
    She started—gave it—she must need.
    " 'Tis not from Mosby? May I read?"

And straight such matter he perused
  That with the Guide he went apart.
The Hospital Steward's turn began:
"Must squeeze this darkey; every tap
  Of knowledge we are bound to start."
    "Garry," she said, "tell all you can
    Of Colonel Mosby—that brave man."

"Dun know much, sare; and missis here
  Know less dan me. But dis I know—"
"Well, what?" "I dun know what I know."
"A knowing answer!" The hump-back coughed,
  Rubbing his yellowish wool like tow.
    "Come—Mosby—tell!" "O dun look so!
    My gal nursed missis—let we go."

"Go where?" demanded Captain Cloud;
  Back into bondage? Man, you're free!"
"Well, *let* we free!" The Captain's brow
Lowered; the Colonel came—had heard:
  "Pooh! pooh! his simple heart I see—
    A faithful servant.—Lady" (a bow),
    "Mosby's abroad—with us you'll go.

"Guard! look to your prisoners; back to camp!
  The man in the grass—can he mount and away?
Why, how he groans!" "Bad inward bruise—
Might lug him along in the ambulance."
  "Coals to Newcastle! let him stay.
    Boots and saddles!—our pains we lose,
    Nor care I if Mosby hear the news!"

But word was sent to a house at hand,
  And a flask was left by the hurt one's side.
They seized in that same house a man,
Neutral by day, by night a foe—
  So charged his neighbor late, the Guide.
    A grudge? Hate will do what it can;
    Along he went for a Mosby-man.

No secrets now; the bugle calls;
  The open road they take, nor shun
The hill; retrace the weary way.
But one there was who whispered low,
  "This is a feint—we'll back anon;
      Young Hair-Brains don't retreat, they say;
      A brush with Mosby is the play!"

They rode till eve. Then on a farm
  That lay along a hill-side green,
Bivouacked. Fires were made, and then
Coffee was boiled; a cow was coaxed
  And killed, and savory roasts were seen;
      And under the lee of a cattle-pen
      The guard supped freely with Mosby's men.

The ball was bandied to and fro;
  Hits were given and hits were met:
"Chickamauga, Feds—take off your hat!"
"But the Fight in the Clouds repaid you, Rebs!"
  "Forgotten about Manassas yet?"
      Chatting and chaffing, and tit for tat,
      Mosby's clan with the troopers sat.

"Here comes the moon!" a captive cried;
  "A song." what say? Archy, my lad!"
Hailing the still one of the clan
(A boyish face with girlish hair),
  "Give us that thing poor Pansy made
      Last year." He brightened, and began;
      And this was the song of Mosby's man:

    Spring is come; she shows her pass—
      Wild violets cool!
    South of woods a small close grass—
      A vernal wool!
    Leaves are a'bud on the sassafras—
      They'll soon be full:
    Blessings on the friendly screen—
    I'm for the South! says the leafage green.

    Robins! fly, and take your fill
      of out-of-doors—

Garden, orchard, meadow, hill,
  Barns and bowers;
Take your fill, and have your will—
  Virginia's yours!
But, bluebirds! keep away, and fear
The ambuscade in bushes here.

"A green song that," a sergeant said;
  "But where's poor Pansy? gone, I fear."
"Ay, mustered out at Ashby's Gap."
"I see; now for a live man's song;
  Ditty for ditty—prepare to cheer.
    Comrades, you can fling a cap!
    You barehead Mosby-boys—why—clap!"

Nine Blue-coats went a-nutting
  Slyly in Tennessee—
Not for chestnuts—better than that—
  Hush, you bumble-bee!
    Nutting, nutting—
    All through the year there's nutting!

A tree they spied so yellow,
  Rustling in motion queer;
In they fired, and down they dropped—
  Butternuts, my dear!
    Nutting, nutting—
    Who'll 'list to go a-nutting?

Ah! why should good fellows foemen be?
  And who would dream that foes they were—
Larking and singing so friendly then—
A family likeness in every face.
  But Captain Cloud made sour demur:
    "Guard! keep your prisoners *in* the pen,
    And let none talk with Mosby's men."

That captain was a valorous one
  (No irony, but honest truth),
Yet down from his brain cold drops distilled,
Making stalactites in his heart—
  A conscientious soul, forsooth;
    And with a formal hate was filled
    Of Mosby's band; and some he'd killed.

Meantime the lady rueful sat,
    Watching the flicker of a fire
Where the Colonel played the outdoor host
In brave old hall of ancient Night.
    But ever the dame grew shyer and shyer,
        Seeming with private grief engrossed—
        Grief far from Mosby, housed or lost.

The ruddy embers showed her pale.
    The Soldier did his best devoir:
"Some coffee?—no?—a cracker?—one?"
Cared for her servant—sought to cheer:
    "I know, I know—a cruel war!
        But wait—even Mosby'll eat his bun;
        The Old Hearth—back to it anon!"

But cordial words no balm could bring;
    She sighed, and kept her inward chafe,
And seemed to hate the voice of glee—
Joyless and tearless. Soon he called
    An escort: "See this lady safe
        In yonder house.—Madam, you're free.
        And now for Mosby.—Guide! with me."

("A night-ride, eh") "Tighten your girths!
    But, buglers! not a note from you.
Fling more rails on the fires—a blaze!"
("Sergeant, a feint—I told you so—
    Toward Aldie again. Bivouac, adieu!")
        After the cherry flames they gaze,
        Then back for Mosby through the maze.

The moon looked through the trees, and tipped
    The scabbards with her elfin beam;
The Leader backward cast his glance,
Proud of the cavalcade that came—
    A hundred horses, bay and cream:
        "Major! look how the lads advance—
        Mosby we'll have in the ambulance!"

"No doubt, no doubt:—was that a hare?—
    First catch, then cook; and cook him brown."
"Trust me to catch," the other cried—
"The lady's letter!—a dance, man, dance

This night is given in Leesburg town!"
   "He'll be there, too!" wheezed out the Guide;
   "That Mosby loves a dance and ride!"

"The lady, ah!—the lady's letter—
  A *lady*, then, is in the case,"
Muttered the Major. "Ay, her aunt
  Writes her to come by Friday eve
  (To-night), for people of the place,
    At Mosby's last fight jubilant,
    A party give, though table-cheer be scant."

The Major hemmed. "Then this night-ride
  We owe to her?—One lighted house
In a town else dark.—The moths, begar!
Are not quite yet all dead!" "How? how?"
   "A mute, meek, mournful little mouse!—
    Mosby has wiles which subtle are—
    But woman's wiles in wiles of war!"

"Tut, Major! by what craft or guile—"
  "Can't tell! but he'll be found in wait.
Softly we enter, say, the town—
Good! pickets post, and all so sure—
   When—crack! the rifles from every gate,   .
    The Grey-backs fire—dash up and down—
    Each alley unto Mosby known!"

"Now, Major, now—you take dark views
  Of a moonlight night." "Well, well, we'll see,"
And smoked as if each whiff were gain.
The other mused; then sudden asked,
   "What would you do in grand decree?"
    "I'd beat, if I could, Lee's armies—then
    Send constables after Mosby's men."

"Ay, ay!—you're odd." The moon sailed up;
  On through the shadowy land they went.
"Names must be made and printed be!"
Hummed the blithe Colonel. "Doc, your flask!
  Major, I drink to your good content.
    My pipe is out—enough for me!
    One's buttons shine—does Mosby see?

"But what comes here?" A man from the front
  Reported a tree athwart the road.
"Go round it, then; no time to bide;
All right—go on! Were one to stay
  For each distrust of a nervous mood,
      Long miles we'd make in this our ride
      Through Mosby-land.—On! with the Guide!"

Then sportful to the Surgeon turned:
  "Green sashes hardly serve by night!"
"Nor bullets nor bottles," the Major sighed,
"Against these moccasin-snakes—such foes
  As seldom come to solid fight:
      They kill and vanish; through grass they glide;
      Devil take Mosby!"—his horse here shied.

"Hold! look—the tree, like a dragged balloon;
  A globe of leaves—some trickery here;
My nag is right—best now be shy."
A movement was made, a hubbub and snarl;
  Little was plain—they blindly steer.
      The Pleiads, as from ambush sly,
      Peep out—Mosby's men in the sky!

As restive they turn, how sore they feel,
  And cross, and sleepy, and full of spleen,
And curse the war. "Fools, North and South!"
Said one right out. "O for a bed!
  O now to drop in this woodland green!"
      He drops as the syllables leave his mouth
      Mosby speaks from the undergrowth—

Speaks in a volley! out jets the flame!
  Men fall from their saddles like plums from trees;
Horses take fright, reins tangle and bind;
"Steady—dismount—form—and into the wood!"
  They go, but find what scarce can please:
      Their steeds have been tied in the field behind,
      And Mosby's men are off like the wind.

Sound the recall! vain to pursue—
  The enemy scatters in wilds he knows,
To reunite in his own good time;

And, to follow, they need divide—
  To come lone and lost on crouching foes:
    Maple and hemlock, beech and lime,
    Are Mosby's confederates, share the crime.

"Major," burst in a bugler small,
  "The fellow we left in Loudon grass—
Sir Slyboots with the inward bruise,
His voice I heard—the very same—
  Some watchword in the ambush pass;
    Ay, sir, we had him in his shoes—
    We caught him—Mosby—but to lose!"

"Go, go!—these saddle-dreamers! Well,
  And here's another.—Cool, sir, cool!"
"Major, I saw them mount and sweep,
And one was bumped, or I mistake,
  And in the skurry dropped his wool."
    "A wig! go fetch it:—the lads need sleep;
    They'll next see Mosby in a sheep!

"Come, come, fall back! reform your ranks—
  All's jackstraws here! Where's Captain Morn?—
We've parted like boats in a raging tide!
But stay—the Colonel—did he charge?
  And comes he there? 'Tis streak of dawn;
    Mosby is off, the woods are wide—
    Hist! there's a groan—this crazy ride!"

As they searched for the fallen, the dawn grew chill;
  They lay in the dew: "Ah, hurt much, Mink?
And—yes—the Colonel!" Dead! but so calm
That death seemed nothing—even death,
  The thing we deem every thing heart can think;
    Amid wilding roses that shed their balm,
    Careless of Mosby he lay—in a charm!

The Major took him by the hand—
  Into the friendly clasp it bled
(A ball through heart and hand he rued):
"Good-bye!" and gazed with humid glance;
  Then in a hollow revery said,
    "The weakest thing is lustihood;
    But Mosby"—and he checked his mood.

"Where's the advance?—cut off, by heaven!
　Come, Surgeon, how with your wounded there?"
"The ambulance will carry all."
"Well, get them in; we go to camp.
　Seven prisoners gone? for the rest have care."
　　Then to himself, "This grief is gall;
　　That Mosby!—I'll cast a silver ball!"

"Ho!" turning—"Captain Cloud, you mind
　The place where the escort went—so shady?
Go, search every closet low and high,
And barn, and bin, and hidden bower—
　Every covert—find that lady!
　　And yet I may misjudge her—ay,
　　Women (like Mosby) mystify.

"We'll see. Ay, Captain, go—with speed!
　Surround and search; each living thing
Secure; that done, await us where
We last turned off. Stay! fire the cage
　If the birds be flown." By the cross-road spring
　　The bands rejoined; no word; the glare
　　Told all. Had Mosby plotted there?

The weary troop that wended now—
　Hardly it seemed the same that pricked
Forth to the forest from the camp:
Foot-sore horses, jaded men;
　Every backbone felt as nicked,
　　Each eye dim as a sick-room lamp,
　　All faces stamped with Mosby's stamp.

In order due the Major rode—
　Chaplain and Surgeon on either hand;
A riderless horse a negro led;
In a wagon the blanketed sleeper went;
　Then the ambulance with the bleeding band;
　　And, an emptied oat-bag on each head,
　　Went Mosby's men, and marked the dead.

What gloomed them? what so cast them down,
　And changed the cheer that late they took,
As double-guarded now they rode
Between the files of moody men?

Some sudden consciousness they brook,
　　Or dread the sequel. That night's blood
　　Disturbed even Mosby's brotherhood.

The flagging horses stumbled at roots,
　　Floundered in mires, or clinked the stones;
No ride spake except aside;
But the wounded cramped in the ambulance,
　　It was horror to hear their groans—
　　　　Jerked along in the woodland ride,
　　　　While Mosby's clan their revery hide.

The Hospital Steward—even he—
　　Who on the sleeper kept his glance,
Was changed; late bright-black beard and eye
Looked now hearse-black; his heavy heart,
　　Like his fagged mare, no more could dance;
　　　　His grape was now a raisin dry:
　　　　'Tis Mosby's homily—*Man must die.*

The amber sunset flushed the camp
　　As on the hill their eyes they fed;
The pickets dumb looks at the wagon dart;
A handkerchief waves from the bannered tent—
　　As white, alas! the face of the dead:
　　　　Who shall the withering news impart?
　　　　The bullet of Mosby goes through heart to heart!

They buried him where the lone ones lie
　　(Lone sentries shot on midnight post)—
A green-wood grave-yard hid from ken,
Where sweet-fern flings an odor nigh—
　　Yet held in fear for the gleaming ghost!
　　　　Though the bride should see threescore and ten,
　　　　She will dream of Mosby and his men.

Now halt the verse, and turn aside—
　　The cypress falls athwart the way;
No joy remains for bard to sing;
And heaviest dole of all is this,
　　That other hearts shall be as gay
　　　　As hers that now no more shall spring:
　　　　To Mosby-land the dirges cling.

LEE IN THE CAPITOL[x]
(April, 1866)

Hard pressed by numbers in his strait
  Rebellion's soldier-chief no more contends—
Feels that the hour is come of Fate,
  Lays down one sword, and widened warfare ends.
The captain who fierce armies led
Becomes a quiet seminary's head—
Poor as his privates, earns his bread.
In studious cares and aims engrossed,
  Strives to forget Stuart and Stonewall dead—
Comrades and cause, station and riches lost,
  And all the ills that flock when fortune's fled.
No word he breathes of vain lament,
  Mute to reproach, nor hears applause—
His doom accepts, perforce content,
  And acquiesces in asserted laws;
Secluded now would pass his life,
And leave to time the sequel of the strife.
  But missives from the Senators ran;
Not that they now would gaze upon a swordless foe,
And power made powerless and brought low:
  Reasons of state, 'tis claimed, require the man.
Demurring not, promptly he comes
By ways which show the blackened homes,
  And—last—the seat no more his own,
But Honor's; patriot grave-yards fill
The forfeit slopes of that patrician hill,
  And fling a shroud on Arlington.
The oaks ancestral all are low;
No more from the porch his glance shall go
Ranging the varied landscape o'er,
Far as the looming Dome—no more.
One look he gives, then turns aside,
Solace he summons from his pride:
"So be it! They await me now
Who wrought this stinging overthrow;
They wait me; not as on the day
Of Pope's impelled retreat in disarray—

By me impelled—when toward yon Dome
The clouds of war came rolling home."
The burst, the bitterness was spent,
The heart-burst bitterly turbulent,
And on he fared.

        In nearness now
He marks the Capitol—a show
Lifted in amplitude, and set
With standards flushed with the glow of Richmond yet;
   Trees and green terraces sleep below.
Through the clear air, in sunny light,
The marble dazes—a temple white.

Intrepid soldier! had his blade been drawn
For yon starred flag, never as now
Bid to the Senate-house had he gone,
But freely, and in pageant borne,
As when brave numbers without number, massed,
Plumed the broad way, and pouring passed—
Bannered, beflowered—between the shores
Of faces, and the dinn'd huzzas,
And balconies kindling at the sabre-flash,
'Mid roar of drums and guns, and cymbal-crash,
While Grant and Sherman shone in blue—
Close of the war and victory's long review.

Yet pride at hand still aidful swelled,
And up the hard ascent he held.
The meeting follows. In his mien
The victor and the vanquished both are seen—
All that he is, and what he late had been.
Awhile, with curious eyes they scan
The Chief who led invasion's van—
Allied by family to one,
Founder of the Arch the Invader warred upon:
Who looks at Lee must think of Washington;
In pain must think, and hide the thought,
So deep with grievous meaning it is fraught.

Secession in her soldier shows
Silent and patient; and they feel
   (Developed even in just success)

Dim inklings of a hazy future steal;
  Their thoughts their questions well express:
"Does the sad South still cherish hate?
Freely will Southern men with Northern mate?
The blacks—should we our arm withdraw,
Would that betray them? some distrust your law.
And how if foreign fleets should come—
Would the South then drive her wedges home?"
And more hereof. The Virginian sees—
Replies to such anxieties.
Discreet his answers run—appear
Briefly straightforward, coldly clear.

"If now," the Senators, closing, say,
"Aught else remain, speak out, we pray."
Hereat he paused; his better heart
Strove strongly then; prompted a worthier part
Than coldly to endure his doom.
Speak out? Ay, speak, and for the brave,
Who else no voice or proxy have;
Frankly their spokesman here become,
And the flushed North from her own victory save.
That inspiration overrode—
Hardly it quelled the galling load
Of personal ill. The inner feud
He, self-contained, a while withstood;
They waiting. In his troubled eye
Shadows from clouds unseen they spy;
They could not mark within his breast
The pang which pleading thought oppressed:
He spoke, nor felt the bitterness die.

"My word is given—it ties my sword;
Even were banners still abroad,
Never could I strive in arms again
While you, as fit, that pledge retain.
Our cause I followed, stood in field and gate—
All's over now, and now I follow Fate.
But this is naught. A People call—
A desolated land, and all
The brood of ills that press so sore,
The natural offspring of this civil war,

Which ending not in fame, such as might rear
Fitly its sculptured trophy here,
Yields harvest large of doubt and dread
To all who have the heart and head
To feel and know. How shall I speak?
Thoughts knot with thoughts, and utterance check.
Before my eyes there swims a haze,
Through mists departed comrades gaze—
First to encourage, last that shall upbraid!
How shall I speak? The South would fain
Feel peace, have quiet law again—
Replant the trees for homestead-shade.
   You ask if she recants: she yields.
Nay, and would more; would blend anew,
As the bones of the slain in her forests do,
Bewailed alike by us and you.
   A voice comes out from those charnel-fields,
A plaintive yet unheeded one:
'Died all in vain? both sides undone?'
Push not your triumph; do not urge
Submissiveness beyond the verge.
Intestine rancor would you bide,
Nursing eleven sliding daggers in your side?
Far from my thought to school or threat;
I speak the things which hard beset.
Where various hazards meet the eyes,
To elect in magnanimity is wise.
Reap victory's fruit while sound the core;
What sounder fruit than re-established law?
I know your partial thoughts do press
Solely on us for war's unhappy stress;
But weigh—consider—look at all,
And broad anathema you'll recall.
The censor's charge I'll not repeat,
That meddlers kindled the war's white heat—
Vain intermeddlers or malign,
Both of the palm and of the pine;
I waive the thought—which never can be rife—
Common's the crime in every civil strife:
But this I feel, that North and South were driven
By Fate to arms. For *our* unshriven,

What thousands, truest souls, were tried—
  As never may any be again—
All those who stemmed Secession's pride,
But at last were swept by the urgent tide
  Into the chasm. I know their pain.
A story here may be applied:
"In Moorish lands there lived a maid
  Brought to confess by vow the creed
  Of Christians. Fain would priests persuade
That now she must approve by deed
  The faith she kept. "What deed?" she asked.
"Your old sire leave, nor deem it sin,
  And come with us." Still more they tasked
The sad one: "If heaven you'd win—
Far from the burning pit withdraw,
Then must you learn to hate your kin,
  Yea, side against them—such the law,
For Moor and Christian are at war."
"Then will I never quit my sire,
But here with him through every trial go,
Nor leave him though in flames below—
God help me in his fire!"
So in the South; vain every plea
'Gainst Nature's strong fidelity;
  True to the home and to the heart,
Throngs cast their lot with kith and kin,
  Foreboding, cleaved to the natural part—
Was this the unforgivable sin?
These noble spirits are yet yours to win.
Shall the great North go Sylla's way?
Proscribe? prolong the evil day?
Confirm the curse? infix the hate?
In Union's name forever alienate?
From reason who can urge the plea—
Freemen conquerors of the free?
When blood returns to the shrunken vein,
Shall the wound of the Nation bleed again?
Well may the wars wan thought supply,
And kill the kindling of the hopeful eye,

Unless you do what even kings have done
In leniency—unless you shun
To copy Europe in her worst estate—
Avoid the tyranny you reprobate."

He ceased. His earnestness unforeseen
Moved, but not swayed their former mien;
   And they dismissed him. Forth he went
Through vaulted walks in lengthened line
Like porches erst upon the Palatine:
   Historic reveries their lesson lent,
   The Past her shadow through the Future sent.

But no. Brave though the Soldier, grave his plea—
   Catching the light in the future's skies,
Instinct disowns each darkening prophecy:
   Faith in America never dies;
Heaven shall the end ordained fulfill.
We march with Providence cheery still.

A MEDITATION

How often in the years that close,
   When truce had stilled the sieging gun,
The soldiers, mounting on their works,
   With mutual curious glance have run
From face to face along the fronting show,
And kinsman spied, or friend—even in a foe.

What thoughts conflicting then were shared,
   While sacred tenderness perforce
Welled from the heart and wet the eye;
   And something of a strange remorse
Rebelled against the sanctioned sin of blood,
And Christian wars of natural brotherhood.

Then stirred the god within the breast—
   The witness that is man's at birth;
A deep misgiving undermined
   Each plea and subterfuge of earth;
They felt in that rapt pause, with warning rife,
Horror and anguish for the civil strife.

Of North or South they recked not then,
   Warm passion cursed the cause of war:
Can Africa pay back this blood
   Spilt on Potomac's shore?
Yet doubts, as pangs, were vain the strife to stay,
And hands that fain had clasped again could slay.

How frequent in the camp was seen
   The herald from the hostile one,
A guest and frank companion there
   When the proud formal talk was done;
The pipe of peace was smoked even 'mid the war,
And fields in Mexico again fought o'er.

In Western battle long they lay
   So near opposed in trench or pit,
That foeman unto foeman called
   As men who screened in tavern sit:

"You bravely fight" each to the other said—
"Toss us a biscuit!" o'er the wall it sped.

And pale on those same slopes, a boy—
    A stormer, bled in noon-day glare;
No aid the Blue-coats then could bring,
    He cried to them who nearest were,
And out there came 'mid howling shot and shell
A daring foe who him befriended well.

Mark the great Captains on both sides,
    The soldiers with the broad renown—
They all were messmates on the Hudson's marge,
    Beneath one roof they laid them down;
And, free from hate in many an after pass,
Strove as in school-boy rivalry of the class.

A darker side there is; but doubt
    In Nature's charity hovers there:
If men for new agreement yearn,
    Then old upbraiding best forbear:
"*The South's the sinner!*" Well, so let it be;
But shall the North sin worse, and stand the Pharisee?

O, now that brave men yield the sword,
    Mine be the manful soldier-view;
By how much more they boldly warred,
    By so much more is mercy due:
When Vicksburg fell, and the moody files marched out,
Silent the victors stood, scorning to raise a shout.

NOTES

NOTE^a

The gloomy lull of the early part of the winter of 1860-1, seeming big with final disaster to our institutions, affected some minds that believed them to constitute one of the great hopes of mankind, much as the eclipse which came over the promise of the first French Revolution affected kindred natures, throwing them for the time into doubts and misgivings universal.

NOTE^b

'The terrible Stone Fleet, on a mission as pitiless as the granite that freights it, sailed this morning from Port Royal, and before two days are past will have made Charleston an inland city. The ships are all old whalers, and cost the Government from $2500 to $5000 each. Some of them were once famous ships.'—(From Newspaper Correspondence of the day.)

Sixteen vessels were accordingly sunk on the bar at the river entrance. Their names were as follows:—

Amazon,	*Leonidas*,
America,	*Maria Theresa*,
American,	*Potomac*,
Archer,	*Rebecca Simms*,
Courier,	*L. C. Richmond*,
Fortune,	*Robin Hood*,
Herald,	*Tenedos*,
Kensington,	*William Lee*.

All accounts seem to agree that the object proposed was not accomplished. The channel is even said to have become ultimately benefited by the means employed to obstruct it.

NOTE^c

The *Temeraire*, that storied ship of the old English fleet, and the subject of the well-known painting by Turner, commends itself to the mind seeking for some one craft to stand for the poetic ideal of those great historic wooden warships, whose gradual displacement is lamented by none more than by regularly educated navy officers, and of all nations.

NOTE^d

Some of the cannon of old times, especially the brass ones, unlike the more effective ordnance of the present day, were cast in shapes which Cellini might have designed, were gracefully enchased, generally with the arms of the country. A few of them—field-pieces—captured in our earlier wars, are preserved in arsenals and navy-yards.

NOTE^e

Whatever just military criticism, favourable or otherwise, has at any time been made upon General McCellan's campaigns, will stand. But if, during the excitement of the conflict, aught was spread abroad tending to unmerited disparagement of the man, it must necessarily die out, though not perhaps without leaving some traces, which may or may not prove enduring. Some there are whose votes aided in the re-election of Abraham Lincoln, who yet believed, and retain the belief, that General McClellan, to say the least, always proved himself a patriotic and honourable soldier. The feeling which surviving comrades entertain for their late commander is one which, from its passion, is susceptible of versified representation, and such it receives.

NOTE^f

At Antietam Stonewall Jackson led one wing of Lee's army, consequently sharing that day in whatever may be deemed to have been the fortunes of his superior.

NOTE^g

Admiral Porter is a son of the late Commodore Porter, commander of the frigate *Essex* on that Pacific cruise which ended in the desperate fight off Valparaiso with the English frigates Cherub and Phoebe, in the year 1814.

NOTE[h]

Among numerous head-stones or monuments on Cemetery Hill, marred or destroyed by th enemy's concentrated fire, was one, somewhat conspicuous, of a Federal officer killed before Richmond in 1862.

On the 4th of July, 1865, the Gettysburg National Cemetery, on the same height with the original burial-ground, was consecrated, and the corner-stone laid of a commemorative pile.

NOTE[i]

'I dare not write the horrible and inconceivable atrocities committed,' says Froissart, in alluding to the remarkable sedition in France during his time. The like may be hinted of some proceedings of the draft-rioters.

NOTE[j]

Although the month was November, the day was in character an October one—cool, clear, bright, intoxicatingly invigorating; one of those days peculiar to the ripest hours of our American autumn. This weather must have had much to do with the spontaneous enthusiasm which seized the troops—an enthusiasm aided, doubtless, by glad thoughts of the victory of Look-out Mountain won the day previous, and also by the elation attending the capture, after a fierce struggle, of the long ranges of rifle-pits at the mountain's base, where orders for the time should have stopped the advance. But there and then it was that the army took the bit between its teeth, and ran away with the generals to the victory commemorated. General Grant, at Culpepper, a few weeks prior to crossing the Rapidan for the Wilderness, expressed to a visitor his impression of the impulse and the spectacle: Said he, 'I never saw anything like it:' language which seems curiously undertoned, considering its application; but from the taciturn Commander it was equivalent to a superlative or hyperbole from the talkative.

The height of the Ridge, according to the account at hand, varies along its length from six to seven hundred feet above the plain; it slopes at an angle of about forty-five degrees.

NOTE[k]

The great Parrott gun, planted in the marshes of James Island, and employed in the prolonged, though at times intermitted bom-

bardment of Charleston, was known among our soldiers as the
Swamp Angel.

St. Michael's, characterised by its venerable tower, was the historic
and aristocratic church of the town.

NOTE[l]

Among the North-western regiments there would seem to have
been more than one which carried a living eagle as an added ensign.
The bird commemorated here was, according to the account, borne
aloft on a perch beside the standard; went through successive
battles and campaigns; was more than once under the surgeon's
hands; and at the close of the contest found honorable repose in
the capital of Wisconsin, from which state he had gone to the wars.

NOTE[m]

The late Major-General McPherson, commanding the Army of
the Tennessee, a native of Ohio and a West Pointer, was one of the
foremost spirits of the war. Young, though a veteran; hardy, in-
trepid, sensitive in honour, full of engaging qualities, with manly
beauty; possessed of genius, a favourite with the army, and with
Grant and Sherman. Both Generals have generously acknowledged
their professional obligations to the able engineer and admirable
soldier, their subordinate and junior.

In an informal account written by the Achilles to this Sarpedon,
he says:

"On that day we avenged his death. Near twenty-two hundred
of the enemy's dead remained on the ground when night closed
upon the scenè of action."

It is significant of the scale on which the war was waged that the
engagement thus written of goes solely (so far as can be learned)
under the vague designation of one of the battles before Atlanta.

NOTE[n]

This piece was written while yet the reports were coming north
of Sherman's homeward advance from Savannah. It is needless to
point out its purely dramatic character.

Though the sentiment ascribed in the beginning of the second
stanza must, in the present reading, suggest the historic tragedy
of the 14th of April, nevertheless, as intimated, it was written prior
to that event, and without any distinct application in the writer's
mind. After consideration, it is allowed to remain.

Few need be reminded that, by the less intelligent classes of the South, Abraham Lincoln, by nature the most kindly of men, was regarded as a monster wantonly warring upon liberty. He stood for the personification of tyrannic power. Each Union soldier was called a Lincolnite.

Undoubtedly Sherman, in the desolation he inflicted after leaving Atlanta, acted not in contravention of orders; and all, in a military point of view, is by military judges deemed to have been expedient, and nothing can abate General Sherman's shining renown; his claims to it rest on no single campaign. Still, there are those who cannot but contrast some of the scenes enacted in Georgia and the Carolinas, and also in the Shenandoah, with a circumstance in a great civil war of heathen antiquity. Plutarch relates that in a military council held by Pompey and the chiefs of that party which stood for the Commonwealth, it was decided that under no plea should any city be sacked that was subject to the people of Rome. There was this difference, however, between the Roman civil conflict and the American one. The war of Pompey and Caesar divided the Roman people promiscuously; that of the North and South ran a frontier line between what for the time were distinct communities or nations. In this circumstance, possibly, and some others, may be found both the cause and the justification of some of the sweeping measures adopted.

NOTE⁰

At this period of excitement the thought was by some passionately welcomed that the Presidential successor had been raised up by heaven to wreak vengeance on the South. The idea originated in the remembrance that Andrew Johnson by birth belonged to that class of Southern whites who never cherished love for the dominant one; that he was a citizen of Tennessee, where the contest at times and in places had been close and bitter as a Middle Age feud; that himself and family had been hardly treated by the Secessionists.

But the expectations built hereon (if, indeed, ever soberly entertained), happily for the country, have not been verified.

Likewise the feeling which would have held the entire South chargeable with the crime of one exceptional assassin, this too has died away with the natural excitement of the hour.

NOTEᴾ

The incident on which this piece is based is narrated in a newspaper account of the battle to be found in the "Rebellion Record."

During the disaster to the National forces on the first day, a brigade on the extreme left found itself isolated. The perils it encountered are given in detail. Among others, the following sentences occur:—

"Under cover of the fire from the bluffs, the rebels rushed down, crossed the ford, and in a moment were seen forming this side the creek in open fields, and within close musket-range. Their colour-bearers stepped defiantly to the front as the engagement opened furiously; the rebels pouring in sharp, quick volleys of musketry, and their batteries above continuing to support them with a destructive fire. Our sharpshooters wanted to pick off the audacious rebel colour-bearers, but Colonel Stuart interposed: "No, no, they're too brave fellows to be killed."

NOTE[q]

According to a report of the Secretary of War, there were on the first day of March, 1865, 965,000 men on the army pay-rolls. Of these, some 200,000—artillery, cavalry, and infantry—made up from the larger portion of the veterans of Grant and Sherman, marched by the President. The total number of Union troops enlisted during the war was 2,668,000.

NOTE[r]

For a month or two after the completion of peace, some thousands of released captives from the military prisons of the North, natives of all parts of the South, passed through the city of New York, sometimes waiting farther transportation for days, during which interval they wandered penniless about the streets, or lay in their worn and patched grey uniforms under the trees of the Battery, near the barracks where they were lodged and fed. They were transported and provided for at the charge of Government.

NOTE[s]

Shortly prior to the evacuation of Petersburg, the enemy, with a view to ultimate repossession, interred some of his heavy guns in the same field with his dead, and with every circumstance calculated to deceive. Subsequently the negroes exposed the stratagem.

NOTE[t]

The records of Northern colleges attest what numbers of our noblest youth went from them to the battle-field. Southern members of the same classes arrayed themselves on the side of Secession;

while Southern seminaries contributed large quotas. Of all these, what numbers marched who never returned except on the shield.

NOTE[u]

Written prior to the founding of the National Cemetery at Andersonville, where 15,000 of the reinterred captives now sleep, each beneath his personal head-board, inscribed from records found in the prison hospital. Some hundreds rest apart and without name. A glance at the published pamphlet containing the list of the buried at Andersonville conveys a feeling mournfully impressive. Seventy-four large double-columned pages in fine print. Looking through them is like getting lost among the old turbaned head-stones and cypresses in the interminable Black Forest of Scutari, over against Constantinople.

NOTE[v]

In one of Kilpatrick's earlier cavalry fights near Aldie, a Colonel who, being under arrest, had been temporarily deprived of his sword, nevertheless, unarmed, insisted upon charging at the head of his men, which he did, and the onset proved victorious.

NOTE[w]

Certain of Mosby's followers, on the charge of being unlicensed foragers or fighters, being hung by order of a Union cavalry commander, the Partisan promptly retaliated in the woods. In turn, this also was retaliated, it is said. To what extent such deplorable proceedings were carried it is not easy to learn.

South of the Potomac in Virginia, and within a gallop of the Long Bridge at Washington, is the confine of a country, in some places wild, which throughout the war it was unsafe for a Union man to traverse except with an armed escort. This was the chase of Mosby, the scene of many of his exploits or those of his men. In the heart of this region at least one fortified camp was maintained by our cavalry, and from time to time expeditions were made therefrom. Owing to the nature of the country and the embittered feeling of its inhabitants, many of these expeditions ended disastrously. Such results were helped by the exceeding cunning of the enemy, born of his woodcraft, and, in some instances, by undue confidence on the part of our men. A body of cavalry, starting from camp with the view of breaking up a nest of rangers, and absent say three days, would return with a number of their own forces killed and wounded (ambushed), without being able to retaliate farther than by foraging on the country, destroying a house or two reported to be haunts of the guerillas, or capturing non-combatants accused of being secretly active in their behalf.

In the verse the name of Mosby is invested with some of those associations with which the popular mind is familiar. But facts do not warrant the belief that every clandestine attack of men who passed for Mosby's was made under his eye, or even by his knowledge.

In partisan warfare he proved himself shrewd, able, and enterprising, and always a wary fighter. He stood well in the confidence of his superior officers, and was employed by them at times in furtherance of important movements. To our wounded on more than one occasion he showed considerate kindness. Officers and civilians captured by forces under his immediate command were, so long as remaining under his orders, treated with civility. These things are well known to those personally familiar with the irregular fighting in Virginia.

NOTE[x]

Among those summoned during the spring just passed to appear before the Reconstruction Committee of Congress was Robert E. Lee. His testimony is deeply interesting, both in itself and as coming from him. After various questions had been put and briefly answered, these words were addressed to him:—

"If there be any other matter about which you wish to speak on this occasion, do so freely." Waiving this invitation, he responded by a short personal explanation of some point in a previous answer, and, after a few more brief questions and replies, the interview closed.

In the verse a poetical liberty has been ventured. Lee is not only represented as responding to the invitation, but also as at last renouncing his cold reserve, doubtless the cloak to feelings more or less poignant. If for such freedom warrant be necessary, the speeches in ancient histories, not to speak of those in Shakespeare's historic plays, may not unfitly perhaps be cited.

The character of the original measures proposed about this time in the National Legislature for the treatment of the (as yet) Congressionally excluded South, and the spirit in which those measures were advocated—these are circumstances which it is fairly supposable would have deeply influenced the thoughts, whether spoken or withheld, of a Southerner placed in the position of Lee before the Reconstruction Committee.

SUPPLEMENT

WERE I fastidiously anxious for the symmetry of this book, it would close with the notes. But the times are such that patriotism—not free from solicitude—urges a claim over-riding all literary scruples.

It is more than a year since the memorable surrender, but events have not yet rounded themselves into completion. Not justly can we complain of this. There has been an upheaval affecting the basis of things; to altered circumstances complicated adaptations are to be made; there are difficulties great and novel. But is Reason still waiting for Passion to spend itself? We have sung of the soldiers and sailors, but who shall hymn the politicians?

In view of the infinite desirableness of Re-establishment, and considering that, so far as feeling is concerned, it depends not mainly on the temper in which the South regards the North, but rather conversely; one who never was a blind adherent feels constrained to submit some thoughts, counting on the indulgence of his countrymen.

And, first, it may be said that, if among the feelings and opinions growing immediately out of a great civil convulsion, there are any which time shall modify or do away, they are presumably those of a less temperate and charitable cast.

There seems no reason why patriotism and narrowness should go together, or why intellectual impartiality should be confounded with political trimming, or why serviceable truth should keep cloistered because not partisan. Yet the work of Reconstruction, if admitted to be feasible at all, demands little but common sense and Christian charity. Little but these? These are much.

Some of us are concerned because as yet the South shows no penitence. But what exactly do we mean by this? Since down to the close of the war she never confessed any for braving it, the only penitence now left her is that which springs solely from the sense of discomfiture; and since this evidently would be a contrition hypocritical, it would be unworthy in us to demand it. Certain it is that penitence, in the sense of voluntary humiliation, will never be displayed. Nor does this afford just ground for unreserved condemnation. It is enough, for all practical purposes, if the South have been taught by the terrors of civil war to feel that Secession, like Slavery, is against Destiny; that both now lie buried in one grave; that her fate is linked with ours; and that together we comprise the Nation.

The clouds of heroes who battled for the Union it is needless to eulogize here. But how of the soldiers on the other side? And when of a free community we name the soldiers, we thereby name the people. It was in subserviency to the slave-interest that Secession was plotted; but it was under the plea, plausibly urged, that certain inestimable rights guaranteed by the Constitution were directly menaced that the people of the South were cajoled into revolution. Through the arts of the conspirators and the perversity of fortune, the most sensitive love of liberty was entrapped into the support of a war whose implied end was the erecting in our advanced century of an Anglo-American empire based upon the systematic degradation of man.

Spite this clinging reproach, however, signal military virtues and achievements have conferred upon the Confederate arms historic fame, and upon certain of the commanders a renown extending beyond the sea—a renown which we of the North could not suppress, even if we would. In personal character, also, not a few of the military leaders of the South enforce forbearance; the memory of others the North refrains from disparaging; and some, with more or less reluctance, she can respect. Posterity, sympathizing with our convictions, but removed from our passions, may perhaps go farther here. If George iv. could, out of the graceful instinct of a gentleman, raise an honourable monument in the great fane of Christendom over the remains of the enemy of his dynasty, Charles Edward, the invader of England and victor in the rout at Preston Pans—upon whose head the king's ancestor but one reign removed had set a price—is it probable that the grandchildren of General Grant will pursue with rancor, or slur by sour neglect, the memory of Stonewall Jackson?

But the South herself is not wanting in recent histories and biographies which record the deeds of her chieftains —writings freely published at the North by loyal houses, widely read here, and with a deep though saddened interest. By students of the war such works are hailed as welcome accessories, and tending to the completeness of the record.

Supposing a happy issue out of present perplexities, then, in the generation next to come, Southerners there will be yielding allegiance to the Union, feeling all their interests bound up in it, and yet cherishing unrebuked that kind of feeling for the memory of the soldiers of the fallen Confederacy that Burns, Scott, and the Ettrick Shepherd felt for the memory of the gallant clansmen ruined through their fidelity to the Stuarts—a feeling whose passion was tempered by the poetry imbuing it, and which in no wise affected their loyalty to the Georges, and which, it may be added, indirectly contributed excellent things to literature. But, setting this view aside, dishonourable would it be in the South were she willing to abandon to shame the memory of brave men who with signal personal disinterestedness warred in her behalf, though from motives, as we believe, so deplorably astray.

Patriotism is not baseness, neither is it inhumanity. The mourners who this summer bear flowers to the mounds of the Virginian and Georgian dead are, in their domestic bereavement and proud affection, as sacred in the eye of Heaven as are those who go with similar offerings of tender grief and love into the cemeteries of our Northern martyrs. And yet, in one aspect, how needless to point the contrast.

Cherishing such sentiments, it will hardly occasion surprise that, in looking over the battle-pieces in the foregoing collection, I have been tempted to withdraw or modify some of them, fearful lest in presenting, though but dramatically and by way of a poetic record, the passions and epithets of civil war, I might be contributing to a bitterness which every sensible American must wish at an end. So, too, with the emotion of victory as reproduced on some pages, and particularly toward the close. It should not be construed into an exultation misapplied—an exultation as ungenerous as unwise, and made to minister, however indirectly, to that kind of censoriousness too apt to be produced in certain

natures by success after trying reverses. Zeal is not of neces-
sity religion, neither is it always of the same essence with
poetry or patriotism.

There were excesses which marked the conflict, most of
which are perhaps inseparable from a civil strife so intense
and prolonged, and involving warfare in some border
countries new and imperfectly civilized. Barbarities also
there were, for which the Southern people collectively
can hardly be held responsible, though perpetrated by
ruffians in their name. But surely other qualities—exalted
ones—courage and fortitude matchless, were likewise dis-
played, and largely; and justly may these be held the charac-
teristic traits, and not the former.

In this view, what Northern writer, however patriotic,
but must revolt from acting on paper a part anyway akin
to that of the live dog to the dead lion; and yet it is right to
rejoice for our triumph, so far as it may justly imply an ad-
vance for our whole country and for humanity.

Let it be held no reproach to any one that he pleads for
reasonable consideration for our late enemies, now stricken
down and unavoidably debarred, for the time, from speak-
ing through authorized agencies for themselves. Nothing
has been urged here in the foolish hope of conciliating those
men—few in number, we trust—who have resolved never
to be reconciled to the Union. On such hearts everything
is thrown away except it be religious commiseration, and
the sincerest. Yet let them call to mind that unhappy Seces-
sionist, not a military man, who with impious alacrity fired
the first shot of the Civil War at Sumter, and a little more
than four years afterward fired the last one into his own heart
at Richmond.

Noble was the gesture into which patriotic passion
surprised the people in a utilitarian time and country;
yet the glory of the war falls short of its pathos—a pathos
which now at last ought to disarm all animosity.

How many and earnest thoughts still rise, and how hard
to repress them. We feel what past years have been, and
years, unretarded years, shall come. May we all have mod-
eration; may we all show candor. Though, perhaps, nothing
could ultimately have averted the strife, and though to treat
of human actions is to deal wholly with second causes, never-

theless, let us not cover up or try to extenuate what, humanly speaking, is the truth—namely, that those unfraternal denunciations, continued through years, and which at last inflamed to deeds that ended in bloodshed, were reciprocal; and that, had the preponderating strength and the prospect of its unlimited increase lain on the other side, on ours might have lain those actions which now in our late opponents we stigmatize under the name of Rebellion. As frankly let us own—what it would be unbecoming to parade were foreigners concerned—that our triumph was won not more by skill and bravery than by superior resources and crushing numbers; that it was a triumph, too, over a people for years politically misled by designing men, and also by some honestly-erring men, who from their position could not have been otherwise than broadly influential; a people who, though, indeed, they sought to perpetuate the curse of slavery, and even extend it, were not the authors of it, but (less fortunate, not less righteous than we) were the fated inheritors; a people who, having a like origin with ourselves, share essentially in whatever worthy qualities we may possess. No one can add to the lasting reproach which hopeless defeat has now cast upon Secession by withholding the recognition of these verities.

Surely we ought to take it to heart that that kind of pacification, based upon principles operating equally all over the land, which lovers of their country yearn for, and which our arms, though signally triumphant, did not bring about, and which law-making, however anxious, or energetic, or repressive, never by itself can achieve, may yet be largely aided by generosity of sentiment public and private. Some revisionary legislation and adaptive is indispensable; but with this should harmoniously work another kind of prudence, not unallied with entire magnanimity. Benevolence and policy—Christianity and Machiavelli—dissuade from penal severities toward the subdued. Abstinence here is as obligatory as considerate care for our unfortunate fellow-men late in bonds, and, if observed, would equally prove to be wise forecast. The great qualities of the South, those attested in the War, we can perilously alienate, or we may make them nationally available at need.

The blacks, in their infant pupilage to freedom, appeal

to the sympathies of every humane mind. The paternal guardianship which for the interval Government exercises over them was prompted equally by duty and benevolence. Yet such kindliness should not be allowed to exclude kindliness to communities who stand nearer to us in nature. For the future of the freed slaves we may well be concerned; but the future of the whole country, involving the future of the blacks, urges a paramount claim upon our anxiety. Effective benignity, like the Nile, is not narrow in its bounty, and true policy is always broad. To be sure, it is vain to seek to glide, with moulded words, over the difficulties of the situation. And for them who are neither partisans, nor enthusiasts, nor theorists, nor cynics, there are some doubts not readily to be solved. And there are fears. Why is not the cessation of war now at length attended with the settled calm of peace? Wherefore in a clear sky do we still turn our eyes toward the South, as the Neapolitan, months after the eruption, turns his toward Vesuvius? Do we dread lest the repose may be deceptive? In the recent convulsion has the crater but shifted? Let us revere that sacred uncertainty which forever impends over men and nations. Those of us who always abhorred slavery as an atheistical iniquity, gladly we join in the exulting chorus of humanity over its downfall. But we should remember that emancipation was accomplished not by deliberate legislation; only through agonized violence could so mighty a result be effected. In our natural solicitude to confirm the benefit of liberty to the blacks, let us forbear from measures of dubious constitutional rightfulness toward our white countrymen—measures of a nature to provoke, among other of the last evils, exterminating hatred of race toward race. In imagination let us place ourselves in the unprecedented position of the Southerners—their position as regards the millions of ignorant manumitted slaves in their midst, for whom some of us now claim the suffrage. Let us be Christians toward our fellow-whites, as well as philanthropists toward the blacks, our fellow-men. In all things, and toward all, we are enjoined to do as we would be done by. Nor should we forget that benevolent desires, after passing a certain point, cannot undertake their own fulfilment without incurring the risk of evils beyond those sought to be remedied. Something may well be left to the graduated care of future legislation, and to heaven. In one point of view the co-existence of the two races in the South—whether the negro be bond or free—seems (even as it did to Abraham Lincoln) a grave evil. Emancipation has ridded the country of the reproach, but not wholly of the calamity. Especially in the present transition period for both races in the South, more or less of trouble may not unreasonably be anticipated; but let us not hereafter be too swift to charge the blame exclusively in any one quarter. With certain evils men must be more or less patient. Our institutions have a potent digestion, and may in time convert and assimilate to good all elements thrown in, however orginally alien.

But, so far as immediate measures looking toward permanent Re-establishment are concerned, no consideration should tempt us to pervert the national victory into oppression for the vanquished. Should plausible promise of eventual good, or a deceptive or spurious sense of duty, lead us to essay this, count we must on serious consequences, not the least of which would be divisions among the Northern adherents of the Union. Assuredly, if any honest Catos there be who thus far have gone with us, no longer will they do so, but oppose us, and as resolutely as hitherto they have supported. But this path of thought leads toward those waters of bitterness from which one can only turn aside and be silent.

But supposing Re-establishment so far advanced that the Southern seats in Congress are occupied, and by men qualified in accordance with those cardinal principles of representative government which hitherto have prevailed in the land—what then? Why, the Congressmen elected by the people of the South will—represent the people of the South. This may seem a flat conclusion; but, in view of the last five years, may there not be latent significance in it? What will be the temper of those Southern members? and, confronted by them, what will be the mood of our own representatives? In private life true reconciliation seldom follows a violent quarrel; but, if subsequent intercourse be unavoidable, nice observances and mutual are indispensable to the prevention of a new rupture. Amity itself can only be maintained by reciprocal respect, and true friends are punctilious equals. On the floor of Congress North and South are to come together after a passionate duel, in which the South, though proving her valor, has been made to bite the dust. Upon differences in debate shall acrimonious recriminations be exchanged? shall censorious superiority assumed by one section provoke defiant self-assertion on the other? shall Manassas and Chickamauga be retorted for Chattanooga and Richmond? Under the supposition that the full Congress will be composed of gentlemen, all this is impossible. Yet, if otherwise, it needs no prophet of Israel to foretell the end. The maintenance of Congressional decency in the future will rest mainly with the North. Rightly will more forbearance be required from the North than the South, for the North is victor.

But some there are who may deem these latter thoughts inapplicable, and for this reason: Since the test-oath operatively excludes from Congress all who in any way participated in Secession, therefore none but Southerners wholly in harmony with the North are eligible to seats. This is true for the time being. But the oath is alterable; and in the wonted fluctuations of parties not improbably it will undergo alteration, assuming such a form, perhaps, as not to bar the admission into the National Legislature of men who represent the populations lately in revolt. Such a result would involve no violation of the principles of democratic government. Not readily can one perceive how the political existence of the millions of late Secessionists can permanently be ignored by this Republic. The years of the war tried our devotion to the Union; the time of peace may test the sincerity of our faith in democracy.

In no spirit of opposition, not by way of challenge, is anything here thrown out. These thoughts are sincere ones; they seem natural—inevitable. Here and there they must have suggested themselves to many thoughtful patriots. And, if they be just thoughts, ere long they must have that weight with the public which already they have had with individuals.

For that heroic band—those children of the furnace who, in regions like Texas and Tennessee, maintained their fidelity through terrible trials—we of the North felt for them, and profoundly we honor them. Yet passionate sympathy, with resentments so close as to be almost domestic in their bitterness, would hardly in the present juncture tend to discreet legislation. Were the Unionists and Secessionists but as Guelphs and Ghibellines? If not, then far be it from a great nation now to act in the spirit that animated a triumphant town-faction in the Middle Ages. But crowding thoughts must at last be checked; and, in times like the present, one who desires to be impartially just in the expression of his views, moves as among sword-points presented on every side.

Let us pray that the terrible historic tragedy of our time may not have been enacted without instructing our whole beloved country through terror and pity; and may fulfilment verify in the end those expectations which kindle the bards of Progress and Humanity.

THE END.

JOHN MARR
AND OTHER SAILORS
WITH SOME SEA PIECES

JOHN MARR

John Marr, toward the close of the last century born in America of a mother unknown, and from boyhood up to maturity a sailor under divers flags, disabled at last from further maritime life by a crippling wound received at close quarters with pirates of the Keys, eventually betakes himself for a livelihood to less active employment ashore. There, too, he transfers his rambling disposition acquired as a sea-farer.

After a variety of removals, at first as a sail-maker from sea-port to sea-port, then adventurously inland as a rough bench-carpenter, he, finally, in the last-named capacity, settles down about the year 1838 upon what was then a frontier-prairie, sparsely sprinkled with small oak-groves and yet fewer log-houses of a little colony but recently from one of our elder inland States. Here, putting a period to his rovings, he marries.

Ere long a fever, the bane of new settlements on teeming loam, and whose sallow livery was certain to show itself, after an interval, in the complexions of too many of these people, carries off his young wife and infant child. In one coffin, put together by his own hands, they are committed with meager rites to the earth—another mound, though a small one, in the wide prairie, not far from where the mound-builders of a race only conjecturable had left their pottery and bones, one common clay, under a strange terrace ser-pentine in form.

With an honest stillness in his general mien—swarthy and black-browed, with eyes that could soften or flash, but never harden, yet disclosing at times a melancholy depth—this kinless man had affections which, once placed, not readily could be dislodged or resigned to a substituted object. Being now arrived at middle-life, he resolves never to quit the soil that holds the only beings ever connected with him by love in the family tie. His log-house he lets to a new-comer, one glad enough to get it, and dwells with the household.

While the acuter sense of his bereavement becomes molli-fied by time, the void at heart abides. Fain, if possible, would he fill that void by cultivating social relations yet nearer than before with a people whose lot he purposes sharing to the end—relations superadded to that mere work-a-day bond arising from participation in the same outward hardships, making reciprocal helpfulness a matter of course. But here, and nobody to blame, he is obstructed.

More familiarly to consort, men of a practical turn must sympathetically converse, and upon topics of real life. But, whether as to persons or events, one cannot always be talking about the present, much less speculating about the future; one must needs recur to the past, which, with the mass of men, where the past is in any personal way a common in-heritance, supplies to most practical natures the basis of sympathetic communion.

But the past of John Marr was not the past of these pioneers. Their hands had rested on the plow-tail, his upon the ship's helm. They knew but their own kind and their own usages; to him had been revealed something of the checkered globe. So limited unavoidably was the mental reach, and by consequence the range of sympathy, in this particular band of domestic emigrants, hereditary tillers of the soil, that the ocean, but a hearsay to their fathers, had now through yet deeper inland removal become to them-selves little more than a rumor traditional and vague.

They were a staid people; staid through habituation to monotonous hardship; ascetics by necessity not less than through moral bias; nearly all of them sincerely, however narrowly, religious. They were kindly at need, after their fashion; but to a man wonted—as John Marr in his previous homeless sojournings could not but have been—to the free-and-easy tavern-clubs affording cheap recreation of an even-ing in certain old and comfortable sea-port towns of that time, and yet more familiar with the companionship afloat of the sailors of the same period, something was lacking. That something was geniality, the flower of life springing from some sense of joy in it, more or less. This their lot could not give to these hard-working endurers of the dispiriting malaria, —men to whom a holiday never came,—and they had too much of uprightness and no art at all or desire to affect what

they did not really feel. At a corn-husking, their least grave
of gatherings, did the lone-hearted mariner seek to divert
his own thoughts from sadness, and in some degree interest
theirs, by adverting to aught removed from the crosses and
trials of their personal surroundings, naturally enough he
would slide into some marine story or picture, but would
soon recoil upon himself and be silent, finding no encourage-
ment to proceed. Upon one such occasion an elderly man—a
blacksmith, and at Sunday gatherings an earnest exhorter—
honestly said to him, "Friend, we know nothing of that here."

Such unresponsiveness in one's fellow-creatures set apart
from factitious life, and by their vocation—in those days little
helped by machinery—standing, as it were, next of kin to
Nature; this, to John Marr, seemed of a piece with the apathy
of Nature herself as envisaged to him here on a prairie where
none but the perished mound-builders had as yet left a
durable mark.

The remnant of Indians thereabout—all but exterminated
in their recent and final war with regular white troops, a
war waged by the Red Men for their native soil and natural
rights—had been coerced into the occupancy of wilds not
very far beyond the Mississippi—wilds *then*, but now the
seats of municipalities and States. Prior to that, the bisons,
once streaming countless in processional herds, or browsing
as in an endless battle-line over these vast aboriginal pas-
tures, had retreated, dwindled in number, before the hunt-
ers, in main a race distinct from the agricultural pioneers,
though generally their advance-guard. Such a double exodus
of man and beast left the plain a desert, green or blossoming
indeed, but almost as forsaken as the Siberian Obi. Save the
prairie-hen, sometimes startled from its lurking-place in the
rank grass; and, in their migratory season, pigeons, high
overhead on the wing, in dense multitudes eclipsing the
day like a passing storm-cloud; save these—there being no
wide woods with their underwood—birds were strangely
few.

Blank stillness would for hours reign unbroken on this
prairie. "It is the bed of a dried-up sea," said the companion-
less sailor—no geologist—to himself, musing at twilight upon
the fixed undulations of that immense alluvial expanse
bounded only by the horizon, and missing there the stir that,

to alert eyes and ears, animates at all times the apparent soli-
tudes of the deep.

But a scene quite at variance with one's antecedents may
yet prove suggestive of them. Hooped round by a level rim,
the prairie was to John Marr a reminder of ocean.

With some of his former shipmates, *chums* on certain
cruises, he had contrived, prior to this last and more remote
removal, to keep up a little correspondence at odd intervals.
But from tidings of anybody or any sort he, in common with
the other settlers, was now cut off; quite cut off, except from
such news as might be conveyed over the grassy billows
by the last-arrived prairie-schooner—the vernacular term, in
those parts and times, for the emigrant-wagon arched high
over with sail-cloth, and voyaging across the vast champaign.
There was no reachable post-office as yet; not even the rude
little receptive box with lid and leather hinges, set up at con-
venient intervals on a stout stake along some solitary green
way, affording a perch for birds, and which, later in the un-
intermitting advance of the frontier, would perhaps decay
into a mossy monument, attesting yet another successive
overleaped limit of civilized life; a life which in America can
to-day hardly be said to have any western bound but the
ocean that washes Asia. Throughout these plains, now in
places overpopulous with towns over-opulent; sweeping
plains, elsewhere fenced off in every direction into flourish-
ing farms—pale townsmen and hale farmers alike, in part,
the descendants of the first sallow settlers; a region that half
a century ago produced little for the sustenance of man, but
to-day launching its superabundant wheat-harvest on the
world;—of this prairie, now everywhere intersected with
wire and rail, hardly can it be said that at the period here
written of there was so much as a traceable road. To the long-
distance traveller the oak-groves, wide apart, and varying
in compass and form; these, with recent settlements, yet
more widely separate, offered some landmarks; but otherwise
he steered by the sun. In early midsummer, even going but
from one log-encampment to the next, a journey it might be
of hours or good part of a day, travel was much like naviga-
tion. In some more enriched depressions between the long,
green, graduated swells, smooth as those of ocean becalmed

receiving and subduing to its own tranquillity the volumin-
ous surge raised by some far-off hurricane of days previous,
here one would catch the first indication of advancing strang-
ers either in the distance, as a far sail at sea, by the glistening
white canvas of the wagon, the wagon itself wading through
the rank vegetation and hidden by it, or, failing that, when
near to, in the ears of the team, peeking, if not above the tall
tiger-lilies, yet above the yet taller grass.

Luxuriant, this wilderness; but, to its denizen, a friend left
behind anywhere in the world seemed not alone absent to
sight, but an absentee from existence.

Though John Marr's shipmates could not all have departed
life, yet as subjects of meditation they were like phantoms
of the dead. As the growing sense of his environment threw
him more and more upon retrospective musings, these phan-
toms, next to those of his wife and child, became spiritual
companions, losing something of their first indistinctness
and putting on at last a dim semblance of mute life; and they
were lit by that aureola circling over any object of the affec-
tions of the past for reunion with which an imaginative heart
passionately yearns.

He invokes these visionary ones,—striving, as it were, to
get into verbal communion with them, or, under yet stronger
illusion, reproaching them for their silence:—

> Since as in night's deck-watch ye show,
> Why, lads, so silent here to me,
> Your watchmate of times long ago?
>
> Once, for all the darkling sea,
> You your voices raised how clearly,
> Striking in when tempest sung;
> Hoisting up the storm-sail cheerly,
> *Life is storm—let storm!* you rung.
> Taking things as fated merely,
> Child-like though the world ye spanned;
> Nor holding unto life too dearly,
> Ye who held your lives in hand—
> Skimmers, who on oceans four
> Petrels were, and larks ashore.

O, not from memory lightly flung,
Forgot, like strains no more availing,
The heart to music haughtier strung;
Nay, frequent near me, never staleing,
Whose good feeling kept ye young.
Like tides that enter creek or stream,
Ye come, ye visit me, or seem
Swimming out from seas of faces,
Alien myriads memory traces,
To enfold me in a dream!

I yearn as ye. But rafts that strain,
Parted, shall they lock again?
Twined we were, entwined, then riven,
Ever to new embracements driven,
Shifting gulf-weed of the main!
And how if one here shift no more,
Lodged by the flinging surge ashore?
Nor less, as now, in eve's decline,
Your shadowy fellowship is mine.
Ye float around me, form and feature:—
Tattooings, ear-rings, love-locks curled;
Barbarians of man's simpler nature,
Unworldly servers of the world.
Yea, present all, and dear to me,
Though shades, or scouring China's sea.

Whither, whither, merchant-sailors,
Whitherward now in roaring gales?
Competing still, ye huntsman-whalers,
In leviathan's wake what boat prevails?
And man-of-war's men, whereaway?
If now no dinned drum beat to quarters
On the wilds of midnight waters—
Foemen looming through the spray;
Do yet your gangway lanterns, streaming,
Vainly strive to pierce below,
When, tilted from the slant plank gleaming,
A brother you see to darkness go?

But, gunmates lashed in shotted canvas,
If where long watch-below ye keep,

Never the shrill *"All hands up hammocks!"*
Breaks the spell that charms your sleep,
And summoning trumps might vainly call,
And booming guns implore—
A beat, a heart-beat musters all,
One heart-beat at heart-core.
It musters. But to clasp, retain;
To see you at the halyards main—
To hear your chorus once again!

BRIDEGROOM DICK
(1876)

Sunning ourselves in October on a day
Balmy as spring, though the year was in decay,
I lading my pipe, she stirring her tea,
My old woman she says to me,
"Feel ye, old man, how the season mellows?"
And why should I not, blessed heart alive,
Here mellowing myself, past sixty-five,
To think o' the May-time o' pennoned young fellows
This stripped old hulk here for years may survive.

Ere yet, long ago, we were spliced, Bonny Blue,
(Silvery it gleams down the moon-glade o' time,
Ah, sugar in the bowl and berries in the prime!)
Coxswain I o' the Commodore's crew,—
Under me the fellows that manned his fine gig,
Spinning him ashore, a king in full fig.
Chirrupy even when crosses rubbed me,
Bridegroom Dick lieutenants dubbed me.
Pleasant at a yarn, Bob O'Linkum in a song,
Diligent in duty and nattily arrayed,
Favored I was, wife, and *fleeted* right along;
And though but a tot for such a tall grade,
A high quartermaster at last I was made.

All this, old lassie, you have heard before,
But you listen again for the sake e'en o' me;

No babble stales o' the good time o' yore
To Joan, if Darby the babbler be.

Babbler?—O' what? Addled brains, they forget!
O—quartermaster I; yes, the signals set,
Hoisted the ensign, mended it when frayed,
Polished up the binnacle, minded the helm,
And prompt every order blithely obeyed.
To me would the officers say a word cheery—
Break through the starch o' the quarter-deck realm;
His coxswain late, so the Commodore's pet.
Ay, and in night-watches long and weary,
Bored nigh to death with the naval etiquette,
Yearning, too, for fun, some younker, a cadet,
Dropping for time each vain bumptious trick,
Boy-like would unbend to Bridegroom Dick.
But a limit there was—a check, d'ye see:
Those fine young aristocrats knew their degree.

Well, stationed aft where their lordships keep,—
Seldom going forward excepting to sleep,—
I, boozing now on by-gone years,
My betters recall along with my peers.
Recall them? Wife, but I see them plain:
Alive, alert, every man stirs again.
Ay, and again on the lee-side pacing,
My spy-glass carrying, a truncheon in show,
Turning at the taffrail, my footsteps retracing,
Proud in my duty, again methinks I go.
And Dave, Dainty Dave, I mark where he stands,
Our trim sailing-master, to time the high-noon,
That thingumbob sextant perplexing eyes and hands,
Squinting at the sun, or twigging o' the moon;
Then, touching his cap to Old Chock-a-Block
Commanding the quarter-deck,—"Sir, twelve o'clock."

Where sails he now, that trim sailing-master,
Slender, yes, as the ship's sky-s'l pole?
Dimly I mind me of some sad disaster—
Dainty Dave was dropped from the navy-roll!
And ah, for old Lieutenant Chock-a-Block—
Fast, wife, chock-fast to death's black dock!

Buffeted about the obstreperous ocean,
Fleeted his life, if lagged his promotion.
Little girl, they are all, all gone, I think,
Leaving Bridegroom Dick here with lids that wink.

Where is Ap Catesby? The fights fought of yore
Famed him, and laced him with epaulets, and more.
But fame is a wake that after-wakes cross,
And the waters wallow all, and laugh *Where's the loss?*
But John Bull's bullet in his shoulder bearing
Ballasted Ap in his long sea-faring.
The middies they ducked to the man who had messed
With Decatur in the gun-room, or forward pressed
Fighting beside Perry, Hull, Porter, and the rest.

Humped veteran o' the Heart-o'-Oak war,
Moored long in haven where the old heroes are,
Never on *you* did the iron-clads jar!
Your open deck when the boarder assailed,
The frank old heroic hand-to-hand then availed.

But where's Guert Gan? Still heads he the van?
As before Vera-Cruz, when he dashed splashing through
The blue rollers sunned, in his brave gold-and-blue,
And, ere his cutter in keel took the strand,
Aloft waved his sword on the hostile land!
Went up the cheering, the quick chanticleering;
All hands vying—all colors flying:
"Cock-a-doodle-doo!" and "Row, boys, row!"
"Hey, Starry Banner!" "Hi, Santa Anna!"—
Old Scott's young dash at Mexico.
Fine forces o' the land, fine forces o' the sea,
Fleet, army, and flotilla—tell, heart o' me,
Tell, if you can, whereaway now they be!

But ah, how to speak of the hurricane unchained—
The Union's strands parted in the hawser over-strained;
Our flag blown to shreds, anchors gone altogether—
The dashed fleet o' States in Secession's foul weather.

Lost in the smother o' that wide public stress,
In hearts, private hearts, what ties there were snapped!
Tell, Hal——vouch, Will, o' the ward-room mess,

On you how the riving thunder-bolt clapped.
With a bead in your eye and beads in your glass,
And a grip o' the flipper, it was part and pass:
"Hal, must it be; Well, if come indeed the shock,
To North or to South, let the victory cleave,
Vaunt it he may on his dung-hill the cock,
But *Uncle Sam's* eagle never crow will, believe."

Sentiment: ay, while suspended hung all,
Ere the guns against Sumter opened there the ball,
And partners were taken, and the red dance began,
War's red dance o' death!—Well, we, to a man,
We sailors o' the North, wife, how could we lag?—
Strike with your kin, and you stick to the flag!
But to sailors o' the South that easy way was barred.
To some, dame, believe (and I speak o' what I know),
Wormwood the trial and the Uzzite's black shard;
And the faithfuller the heart, the crueller the throe.
Duty? It pulled with more than one string,
This way and that, and anyhow a sting.
The flag and your kin, how be true unto both?
If one plight ye keep, then ye break the other troth.
But elect here they must, though the casuists were out;
Decide—hurry up—and throttle every doubt.

Of all these thrills thrilled at keelson, and throes,
Little felt the shoddyites a-toasting o' their toes;
In mart and bazar Lucre chuckled the huzza,
Coining the dollars in the bloody mint of war.
But in men, gray knights o' the Order o' Scars,
And brave boys bound by vows unto Mars,
Nature grappled honor, intertwisting in the strife:—
But some cut the knot with a thoroughgoing knife.
For how when the drums beat? How in the fray
In Hampton Roads on the fine balmy day?

There a lull, wife, befell—drop o' silence in the din.
Let us enter that silence ere the belchings re-begin.—
Through a ragged rift aslant in the cannonade's smoke
An iron-clad reveals her repellent broadside
Bodily intact. But a frigate, all oak,
Shows honeycombed by shot, and her deck crimson-dyed.

And a trumpet from port of the iron-clad hails,
Summoning the other, whose flag never trails:
"Surrender that frigate, Will! Surrender,
Or I will sink her—*ram*, and end her!"

'T was Hal. And Will, from the naked heart-o'-oak,
Will, the old messmate, minus trumpet, spoke,
Informally intrepid,—"Sink her, and be damned!"
Enough. Gathering way, the iron-clad *rammed*.
The frigate, heeling over, on the wave threw a dusk.
Not sharing in the slant, the clapper of her bell
The fixed metal struck—uninvoked struck the knell
Of the *Cumberland* stilettoed by the *Merrimac's* tusk;
While, broken in the wound underneath the gun-deck,
Like a sword-fish's blade in leviathan waylaid,
The tusk was left infixed in the fast-foundering wreck.
There, dungeoned in the cockpit, the wounded go down,
And the chaplain with them. But the surges uplift
The prone dead from deck, and for moment they drift
Washed with the swimmers, and the spent swimmers drown.
Nine fathom did she sink,—erect, though hid from light
Save her colors unsurrendered and spars that kept the height.

Nay, pardon, old aunty! Wife, never let it fall,
That big started tear that hovers on the brim;
I forgot about your nephew and the *Merrimac's* ball;
No more then of her, since it summons up him.

But talk o' fellows' hearts in the wine's genial cup:—
Trap them in the fate, jamb them in the strait,
Guns speak their hearts then, and speak right up.

The troublous colic o' intestine war
Its sets the bowels o' affection ajar.
But, lord, old dame, so spins the whizzing world,
A humming-top, ay, for the little boy-gods
Flogging it well with their smart little rods,
Tittering at time and the coil uncurled.

Now, now, sweetheart, you sidle away,
No, never you like *that* kind o' *gay;*
But sour if I get, giving truth her due,
Honey-sweet forever, wife, will Dick be to *you!*

But avast with the War! Why recall racking days
Since set up anew are the ship's started stays?
Nor less, though the gale we have left behind,
Well may the heave o' the sea remind.
It irks me now, as it troubled me then,
To think o' the fate in the madness o' men.
If Dick was with Farragut on the night-river,
When the boom-chain we burst in the fire-raft's glare,
That blood-dyed the visage as red as the liver;
In the *Battle for the Bay* too if Dick had a share,
And saw one aloft a-piloting the war—
Trumpet in the whirlwind, a Providence in place—
Our Admiral old whom the captains huzza,
Dick joys in the man nor brags about the race.

But better, wife, I like to booze on the days
Ere the Old Order foundered in these very frays,
And tradition was lost and we learned strange ways.
Often I think on the brave cruises then;
Re-sailing them in memory, I hail the press o'men
On the gunned promenade where rolling they go,
Ere the dog-watch expire and break up the show.
The Laced Caps I see between forward guns;
Away from the powder-room they puff the cigar;
"Three days more, hey, the donnas and the dons!"
"Your Xeres widow, will you hunt her up, Starr?"
The Laced Caps laugh, and the bright waves too;
Very jolly, very wicked, both sea and crew,
Nor heaven looks sour on either, I guess,
Nor Pecksniff he bosses the gods' high mess.

Wistful ye peer, wife, concerned for my head,
And how best go get me betimes to my bed.

But king o' the club, the gayest golden spark,
Sailor o' sailors, what sailor do I mark?
Tom Tight, Tom Tight, no fine fellow finer,
A cutwater-nose, ay, a spirited soul;
But, boozing away at the well-brewed bowl,
He never bowled back from that voyage to China.
Tom was lieutenant in the brig-o'-war famed
When an officer was hung for an arch-mutineer,
But a mystery cleaved, and the captain was blamed,

And a rumpus too raised, though his honor it was clear.
And Tom he would say, when the mousers would try him,
And with cup after cup o' Burgundy ply him:
"Gentlemen, in vain with your wassail you beset,
For the more I tipple, the tighter do I get."
No blabber, no, not even with the can—
True to himself and loyal to his clan.

Tom blessed us starboard and d—d us larboard,
Right down from rail to the streak o' the garboard.
Nor less, wife, we liked him.—Tom was a man
In contrast queer with Chaplain Le Fan,
Who blessed us at morn, and at night yet again,
D—ning us only in decorous strain;
Preaching 'tween the guns—each cutlass in its place—
From text that averred old Adam a hard case.
I see him—Tom—on *horse-block* standing,
Trumpet at mouth, thrown up all amain,
An elephant's bugle, vociferous demanding
Of topmen aloft in the hurricane of rain,
"Letting that sail there your faces flog?
Manhandle it, men, and you'll get the good grog!"
O Tom, but he knew a blue-jacket's ways,
And how a lieutenant may genially haze;
Only a sailor sailors heartily praise.

Wife, where be all these chaps, I wonder?
Trumpets in the tempest, terrors in the fray,
Boomed their commands along the deck like thunder;
But silent is the sod, and thunder dies away.

But Captain Turret, *"Old Hemlock"* tall,
(A leaning tower when his tank brimmed all,)
Manoeuvre out alive from the war did he?
Or, too old for that, drift under the lee?
Kentuckian colossal, who, touching at Madeira,
The huge puncheon shipped o' prime *Santa-Clara;*
Then rocked along the deck so solemnly!
No wit the less though judicious was enough
In dealing with the Finn who made the great huff;
Our three-decker's giant, a grand boatswain's mate,
Manliest of men in his own natural senses;
But driven stark mad by the devil's drugged stuff,

Storming all aboard from his run-ashore late,
Challenging to battle, vouchsafing no pretenses,
A reeling King Ogg, delirious in power,
The quarter-deck carronades he seemed to make cower.
"Put him in *brig* there!" said Lieutenant Marrot.
"Put him in *brig!*" back he mocked like a parrot;
"Try it, then!" swaying a fist like Thor's sledge,
And making the pigmy constables hedge—
Ship's corporals and the master-at-arms.
"In *brig* there, I say!"—They dally no more;
Like hounds let slip on a desperate boar,
Together they pounce on the formidable Finn,
Pinion and cripple and hustle him in.
Anon, under sentry, between twin guns,
He slides off in drowse, and the long night runs.

Morning brings a summons. Whistling it calls,
Shrilled through the pipes of the boatswain's four aids;
Trilled down the hatchways along the dusk halls:
Muster to the Scourge!—Dawn of doom and its blast!
As from cemeteries raised, sailors swarm before the mast,
Tumbling up the ladders from the ship's nether shades.

Keeping in the background and taking small part,
Lounging at their ease, indifferent in face,
Behold the trim marines uncompromised in heart;
Their Major, buttoned up, near the staff finds room—
The staff o' lieutenants standing grouped in their place.
All the Laced Caps o' the ward-room come,
The Chaplain among them, disciplined and dumb.
The blue-nosed boatswain, complexioned like slag,
Like a blue Monday shows—his implements in bag.
Executioners, his aids, a couple by him stand,
At a nod there the thongs to receive from his hand.
Never venturing a caveat whatever may betide,
Though functionally here on humanity's side,
The grave Surgeon shows, like the formal physician
Attending the rack o'the Spanish Inquisition.

The angel o' the "brig" brings his prisoner up;
Then, steadied by his old *Santa-Clara*, a sup,
Heading all erect, the ranged assizes there,
Lo, Captain Turret, and under starred bunting,

(A florid full face and fine silvered hair,)
Gigantic the yet greater giant confronting.

Now the culprit he liked, as a tall captain can
A Titan subordinate and true *sailor-man;*
And frequent he'd shown it—no worded advance,
But flattering the Finn with a well-timed glance.
But what of that now? In the martinet-mien
Read the *Articles of War,* heed the naval routine;
While, cut to the heart a dishonor there to win,
Restored to his senses, stood the Anak Finn;
In racked self-control the squeezed tears peeping,
Scalding the eye with repressed inkeeping.
Discipline must be; the scourge is deemed due.
But ah for the sickening and strange heart-benumbing,
Compassionate abasement in shipmates that view;
Such a grand champion shamed there succumbing!

"Brown, tie him up."—The cord he brooked:
How else?—his arms spread apart—never threaping;
No, never he flinched, never sideways he looked,
Peeled to the waistband, the marble flesh creeping,
Lashed by the sleet the officious winds urge.
In function his fellows their fellowship merge—
The twain standing high—the two boatswain's mates,
Sailors of his grade, ay, and brothers of his mess.
With sharp thongs adroop the junior one awaits
The word to uplift.

                    "Untie him—so!
Submission is enough, Man, you may go."
Then, promenading aft, brushing fat Purser Smart,
"Flog? Never meant it—hadn't any heart.
Degrade that tall fellow?"—Such, wife, was he,
Old Captain Turret, who the brave wine could stow.
Magnanimous, you think?—but what does Dick see?
Apron to your eye! Why, never fell a blow,
Cheer up, old wifie, 't was a long time ago.

But where's that sore one, crabbed and severe,
Lieutenant Long Lumbago, an arch scrutineer?
Call the roll to-day, would he answer—*Here!*
When the *Blixum's* fellows to quarters mustered

How he'd lurch along the lane of gun-crews clustered,
Testy as touchwood, to pry and to peer.
Jerking his sword underneath larboard arm,
He ground his worn grinders to keep himself calm.
Composed in his nerves, from the fidgets set free,
Tell, Sweet Wrinkles, alive now is he,
In Paradise a parlor where the even tempers be?

Where's Commander All-a-Tanto?
Where's Orlop Bob singing up from below?
Where's Rhyming Ned? has he spun his last canto?
Where's Jewsharp Jim? Where's Rigadoon Joe?
Ah, for the music over and done,
The band all dismissed save the droned trombone!
Where's Glen o' the gun-room, who loved Hot-Scotch—
Glen, prompt and cool in a perilous watch?
Where's flaxen-haired Phil? a gray lieutenant?
Or rubicund, flying a dignified pennant?
But where sleeps his brother?—the cruise it was o'er,
But ah, for death's grip that welcomed him ashore!
Where's Sid, the cadet, so frank in his brag,
Whose toast was audacious—*"Here's Sid, and Sid's flag!"*
Like holiday-craft that have sunk unknown,
May a lark of a lad go lonely down?
Who takes the census under the sea?
Can others like old ensigns be,
Bunting I hoisted to flutter at the gaff—
Rags in end that once were flags
Gallant streaming from the staff?
Such scurvy doom could the chances deal
To Top-Gallant Harry and Jack Genteel?
Lo, Genteel Jack in hurricane weather,
Shagged like a bear, like a red lion roaring;
But O, so fine in his chapeau and feather,
In port to the ladies never once *jawing;*
All bland *politesse,* how urbane was he—
"Oui, mademoiselle"—*"Ma chère amie!"*

'T was Jack got up the ball at Naples,
Gay in the old *Ohio* glorious;

His hair was curled by the berth-deck barber,
Never you'd deemed him a cub of rude Boreas;
In tight little pumps, with the grand dames in rout,
A-flinging his shapely foot all about;
His watch-chain with love's jeweled tokens abounding,
Curls ambrosial shaking out odors,
Waltzing along the batteries, astounding
The gunner glum and the grim-visaged loaders.

Wife, where be all these blades, I wonder,
Pennoned fine fellows, so strong, so gay?
Never their colors with a dip dived under;
Have they hauled them down in a lack-lustre day,
Or beached their boats in the Far, Far Away?

Hither and thither, blown wide asunder,
Where's this fleet, I wonder and wonder.
Slipt their cables, rattled their adieu,
(Whereaway pointing? to what rendezvous?)
Out of sight, out of mind, like the crack *Constitution*,
And many a keel time never shall renew—
Bon Homme Dick o'the buff Revolution,
The *Black Cockade* and the staunch *True-Blue*.

Doff hats to Decatur! But where is his blazon?
Must merited fame endure time's wrong—
Glory's ripe grape wizen up to a raisin?
Yes! for Nature teems, and the years are strong,
And who can keep the tally o' the names that fleet along!

But his frigate, wife, his bride? Would blacksmiths brown
Into smithereens smite the solid old renown?

Rivetting the bolts in the iron-clad's shell,
Hark to the hammers with a *rat-tat-tat*;
"Handier a *derby* than a laced cocked hat!
The *Monitor* was ugly, but she served us right well,
Better than the *Cumberland*, a beauty and the belle."

Better than the Cumberland!—Heart alive in me!
That battlemented hull, Tantallon o' the sea,
Kicked in, as at Boston the taxed chests o'tea!

Ay, spurned by the *ram*, once a tall, shapely craft,
But lopped by the *Rebs* to an iron-beaked raft—
A blacksmith's unicorn armed *cap-a-pie*.

Under the water-line a *ram's* blow is dealt:
And foul fall the knuckles that strike below the belt.
Nor brave the inventions that serve to replace
The openness of valor while dismantling the grace.

Aloof from all this and the never-ending game,
Tantamount to teetering, plot and counterplot;
Impenetrable armor—all-perforating shot;
Aloof, bless God, ride the war-ships of old,
A grand fleet moored in the roadstead of fame;
Not submarine sneaks with *them* are enrolled;
Their long shadows dwarf us, their flags are as flame.

Don't fidget so, wife; an old man's passion
Amounts to no more than this smoke that I puff;
There, there now, buss me in good old fashion;
A died-down candle will flicker in the snuff.

But one last thing let your old babbler say,
What Decatur's coxswain said who was long ago hearsed,
"Take in your flying-kites, for there comes a lubber's day
When gallant things will go, and the three-deckers first."

My pipe is smoked out, and the grog runs slack;
But bowse away, wife, at your blessed Bohea;
This empty can here must needs solace me—
Nay, sweetheart, nay; I take that back;
Dick drinks from your eyes and he finds no lack!

TOM DEADLIGHT
(1810)

During a tempest encountered homeward-bound from the
Mediterranean, a grizzled petty-officer, one of the two cap-
tains of the forecastle, dying at night in his hammock, swung
in the *sick-bay* under the tiered gun-decks of the British

Dreadnought, 98, wandering in his mind, though with glimpses of sanity, and starting up at whiles, sings by snatches his good-bye and last injunctions to two messmates, his watchers, one of whom fans the fevered tar with the flap of his old sou'-wester. Some names and phrases, with here and there a line, or part of one; these, in his aberration, wrested into incoherency from their original connection and import, he involuntarily derives, as he does the measure, from a famous old sea-ditty, whose cadences, long rife, and now humming in the collapsing brain, attune the last flutterings of distempered thought.

Farewell and adieu to you noble hearties,—
  Farewell and adieu to you ladies of Spain,
For I've received orders for to sail for the Deadman,
  But hope with the grand fleet to see you again.

I have hove my ship to, with main-top-sail aback, boys;
  I have hove my ship to, for to strike soundings clear—
The black scud a'flying; but, by God's blessing, dam' me,
  Right up the Channel for the Deadman I'll steer.

I have worried through the waters that are callèd the
      Doldrums,
  And growled at Sargasso that clogs while ye grope—
Blast my eyes, but the light-ship is hid by the mist, lads:—
  Flying Dutchman—odds bobbs—off the Cape of Good
      Hope!

But what's this I feel that is fanning my cheek, Matt?
  The white goney's wing?—how she rolls!—'t is the Cape!
Give my kit to the mess, Jock, for kin none is mine, none;
  And tell *Holy Joe* to avast with the crape.

Dead reckoning, says *Joe*, it won't do to go by;
  But they doused all the glims, Matt, in sky t' other night.
Dead reckoning is good for to sail for the Deadman;
  And Tom Deadlight he thinks it may reckon near right.

The signal!—it streams for the grand fleet to anchor.
  The captains—the trumpets—the hullabaloo!
Stand by for blue-blazes, and mind your shank-painters,
  For the Lord High Admiral, he's squinting at you!

But give me my *tot*, Matt, before I roll over;
  Jock, let's have your flipper, it's good for to feel;
And don't sew me up without *baccy* in mouth, boys,
  And don't blubber like lubbers when I turn up my keel.

JACK ROY

Kept up by relays of generations young
Never dies at halyards the blithe chorus sung;
While in sands, sounds, and seas where the storm-petrels cry,
Dropped mute around the globe, these halyard singers lie.
Short-lived the clippers for racing-cups that run,
And speeds in life's career many a lavish mother's-son.

But thou, manly king o' the old *Splendid's* crew,
The ribbons o' thy hat still a-fluttering, should fly—
A challenge, and forever, nor the bravery should rue.
Only in a tussle for the starry flag high,
When 't is piety to do, and privilege to die.
Then, only then, would heaven think to lop   .
Such a cedar as the captain o' the *Splendid's* main-top:
A belted sea-gentleman; a gallant, off-hand
Mercutio indifferent in life's gay command.
Magnanimous in humor; when the splintering shot fell,
"Tooth-picks a-plenty, lads; thank 'em with a shell!"

Sang Larry o' the Cannakin, smuggler o' the wine,
At mess between guns, lad in jovial recline:
"In Limbo our Jack he would chirrup up a cheer,
The martinet there find a chaffing mutineer;
From a thousand fathoms down under hatches o' your Hades,
He'd ascend in love-ditty, kissing fingers to your ladies!"

Never relishing the knave, though allowing for the menial,
Nor overmuch the king, Jack, nor prodigally genial.
Ashore on liberty he flashed in escapade,
Vaulting over life in its levelness of grade,
Like the dolphin off Africa in rainbow a-sweeping—
Arch iridescent shot from seas languid sleeping.

Larking with thy life, if a joy but a toy,
Heroic in thy levity wert thou, Jack Roy.

Sea Pieces

THE HAGLETS

By chapel bare, with walls sea-beat
The lichened urns in wilds are lost
About a carved memorial stone
That shows, decayed and coral-mossed,
A form recumbent, swords at feet,
Trophies at head, and kelp for a winding-sheet.

I invoke thy ghost, neglected fane,
Washed by the waters' long lament;
I adjure the recumbent effigy
To tell the cenotaph's intent—
Reveal why fagotted swords are at feet,
Why trophies appear and weeds are the winding-sheet.

By open ports the Admiral sits,
And shares repose with guns that tell
Of power that smote the arm'd Plate Fleet
Whose sinking flag-ship's colors fell;
But over the Admiral floats in light
His squadron's flag, the red-cross Flag of the White.
        The eddying waters whirl astern,
The prow, a seedsman, sows the spray;
With bellying sails and buckling spars
The black hull leaves a Milky Way;
Her timbers thrill, her batteries roll,
She revelling speeds exulting with pennon at pole,
        But ah, for standards captive trailed
For all their scutcheoned castles' pride—
Castilian towers that dominate Spain,
Naples, and either Ind beside;
Those haughty towers, armorial ones,
Rue the salute from the Admiral's dens of guns.

Ensigns and arms in trophy brave,
Braver for many a rent and scar,
The captor's naval hall bedeck,
Spoil that insures an earldom's star—
Toledoes great, grand draperies too,

Spain's steel and silk, and splendors from Peru.
    But crippled part in splintering fight,
The vanquished flying the victor's flags,
With prize-crews, under convoy-guns,
Heavy the fleet from Opher drags—
The Admiral crowding sail ahead,
Foremost with news who foremost in conflict sped.
    But out from cloistral gallery dim,
In early night his glance is thrown;
He marks the vague reserve of heaven,
He feels the touch of ocean lone;
Then turns, in frame part undermined,
Nor notes the shadowing wings that fan behind.

There, peaked and gray, three haglets fly,
And follow, follow fast in wake
Where slides the cabin-lustre shy,
And sharks from man a glamour take,
Seething along the line of light
In lane that endless rules the war-ship's flight.
    The sea-fowl here, whose hearts none know,
They followed late the flag-ship quelled,
(As now the victor one) and long
Above her gurgling grave, shrill held
With screams their wheeling rites—then sped
Direct in silence where the victor led.
    Now winds less fleet, but fairer, blow,
A ripple laps the coppered side,
While phosphor sparks make ocean gleam,
Like camps lit up in triumph wide;
With lights and tinkling cymbals meet
Acclaiming seas the advancing conqueror greet.

But who a flattering tide may trust,
Or favoring breeze, or aught in end?—
Careening under startling blasts
The sheeted towers of sails impend;
While, gathering bale, behind is bred
A livid storm-bow, like a rainbow dead.
    At trumpet-call the topmen spring;
And, urged by after-call in stress,
Yet other tribes of tars ascend

The rigging's howling wilderness;
But ere yard-ends alert they win,
Hell rules in heaven with hurricane-fire and din.
    The spars, athwart as spiry height,
Like quaking Lima's crosses rock;
Like bees the clustering sailors cling
Against the shrouds, or take the shock
Flat on the swept yard-arms aslant,
Dipped like the wheeling condor's pinions gaunt.

A lull! and tongues of languid flame
Lick every boom, and lambent show
Electric 'gainst each face aloft;
The herds of clouds with bellowings go:
The black ship rears—beset—harassed,
Then plunges far with luminous antlers vast.
    In trim betimes they turn from land,
Some shivered sails and spars they stow;
One watch, dismissed, they troll the can,
While loud the billow thumps the bow—
Vies with the fist that smites the board,
Obstreperous at each reveller's jovial words.
    Of royal oak by storms confirmed,
The tested hull her lineage shows:
Vainly the plungings whelm her prow—
She rallies, rears, she sturdier grows;
Each shot-hole plugged, each storm-sail home,
With batteries housed she rams the watery dome.

Dim seen adrift through driving scud,
The wan moon shows in plight forlorn;
Then, pinched in visage, fades and fades
Like to the faces drowned at morn,
When deeps engulfed the flag-ship's crew,
And, shrilling round, the inscrutable haglets flew.
    And still they fly, nor now they cry,
But constant fan a second wake,
Unflagging pinions ply and ply,
Abreast their course intent they take;
Their silence marks a stable mood,
They patient keep their eager neighborhood.
    Plumed with a smoke, a confluent sea,

Heaved in a combing pyramid full,
Spent at its climax, in collapse
Down headlong thundering stuns the hull:
The trophy drops; but, reared again,
Shows Mars' high-altar and contemns the main.

Rebuilt it stands, the brag of arms,
Transferred in site—no thought of where
The sensitive needle keeps its place,
And starts, disturbed, a quiverer there;
The helmsman rubs the clouded glass—
Peers in, but lets the trembling portent pass.
    Let pass as well his shipmates do
(Whose dream of power no tremors jar)
Fears for the fleet convoyed astern:
"Our flag they fly, they share our star;
Spain's galleons great in hull are stout:
Manned by our men—like us they'll ride it out."
    Tonight's the night that ends the week—
Ends day and week and month and year:
A fourfold imminent flickering time,
For now the midnight draws anear:
Eight bells! and passing-bells they be—
The Old year fades, the Old year dies at sea.

He launched them well. But shall the New
Redeem the pledge the Old Year made,
Or prove a self-asserting heir?
But healthy hearts few qualms invade:
By shot-chests grouped in bays 'tween guns
The gossips chat, the grizzled, sea-beat ones.
    And boyish dreams some graybeards blab:
"To sea, my lads, we go no more
Who share the Acapulco prize;
We'll all night in, and bang the door;
Our ingots red shall yield us bliss:
Lads, golden years begin to-night with this!"
    Released from deck, yet waiting call,
Glazed caps and coats baptized in storm,
A watch of Laced Sleeves round the board
Draw near in heart to keep them warm:
"Sweethearts and wives!" clink, clink, they meet,
And, quaffing, dip in wine their beards of sleet.

"Ay, let the star-light stay withdrawn,
So here her hearth-light memory fling,
So in this wine-light cheer be born,
And honor's fellowship weld our ring—
Honor! our Admiral's aim foretold:
A tomb or a trophy, and lo, 't is a trophy and gold!"
    But he, a unit, sole in rank,
Apart needs keep his lonely state,
The sentry at his guarded door
Mute as by vault the sculptured Fate;
Belted he sits in drowsy light,
And, hatted, nods—the Admiral of the White.
    He dozes, aged with watches passed—
Years, years of pacing to and fro;
He dozes, nor attends the stir
In bullioned standards rustling low,
Nor minds the blades whose secret thrill
Perverts overhead the magnet's Polar will;—

Less heeds the shadowing three that ply
And follow, follow fast in wake,
Untiring wing and lidless eye—
Abreast their course intent they take;
Or sigh or sing, they hold for good
The unvarying flight and fixed inveterate mood.
    In dream at last his dozings merge,
In dream he reaps his victory's fruit:
The Flags-o'-the-Blue, the Flags-o'-the-Red,
Dipped flags of his country's fleets salute
His Flag-o'-the-White in harbor proud——
But why should it blench? Why turn to a painted shroud?
    The hungry seas they hound the hull,
The sharks they dog the haglets' flight;
With one consent the winds, the waves
In hunt with fins and wings unite,
While drear the harps in cordage sound
Remindful wails for old Armadas drowned.

Ha—yonder! are they Northern Lights?
Or signals flashed to warn or ward?
Yea, signals lanced in breakers high;
But doom on warning follows hard:
While yet they veer in hope to shun,

They strike! and thumps of hull and heart are one.
  But beating hearts a drum-beat calls
And prompt the men to quarters go;
Discipline, curbing nature, rules—
Heroic makes who duty know:
They execute the trump's command,
Or in peremptory places wait and stand.
    Yet cast about in blind amaze—
As through their watery shroud they peer:
"We tacked from land: then how betrayed?
Have currents swerved us—snared us here?"
None heed the blades that clash in place
Under lamps dashed down that lit the magnet's case.

Ah, what may live, who mighty swim,
Or boat-crew reach that shore forbid,
Or cable span? Must victors drown—
Perish, even as the vanquished did?
Man keeps from man the stifled moan;
They shouldering stand, yet each in heart how lone.
    Some heaven invoke; but rings of reefs
Prayer and despair alike deride
In dance of breakers forked or peaked,
Pale maniacs of the maddened tide;
While, strenuous yet some end to earn,
The haglets spin, though now no more astern.
    Like shuttles hurrying in the looms
Aloft through rigging frayed they ply—
Cross and recross—weave and inweave,
Then lock the web with clinching cry
Over the seas on seas that clasp
The weltering wreck where gurgling ends the gasp.

Ah for the Plate-Fleet trophy now
The victor's voucher, flags and arms;
Never they'll hang in Abbey old
And take Time's dust with holier palms;
Nor less content, in liquid night,
Their captor sleeps—the Admiral of the White.

    Imbedded deep with shells
    And drifted treasure deep,

Forever he sinks deeper in
Unfathomable sleep—
His cannon round him thrown,
His sailors at his feet,
The wizard sea enchanting them
Where never haglets beat.

On nights when meteors play
And light the breakers dance,
The Oreads from the caves
With silvery elves advance;
And up from ocean stream,
And down from heaven far,
The rays that blend in dream
The abysm and the star.

THE AEOLIAN HARP
AT THE SURF INN

List the harp in window wailing
   Stirred by fitful gales from sea:
Shrieking up in mad crescendo—
   Dying down in plaintive key!

Listen: less a strain ideal
  Than Ariel's rendering of the Real.
What that Real is, let hint
  A picture stamped in memory's mint.

Braced well up, with beams aslant,
Betwixt the continents sails the *Phocion*,
To Baltimore bound from Alicant.
Blue breezy skies white fleeces fleck
Over the chill blue white-capped ocean:
From yard-arm comes—"Wreck ho, a wreck!"

Dismasted and adrift,
Long time a thing forsaken;
Overwashed by every wave
Like the slumbering kraken;

Heedless if the billow roar,
Oblivious of the lull,
Leagues and leagues from shoal or shore,
It swims—a levelled hull:
Bulwarks gone—a shaven wreck,
Nameless, and a grass-green deck.
A lumberman: perchance, in hold
Prostrate pines with hemlocks rolled.

It has drifted, waterlogged,
Till by trailing weeds beclogged:
   Drifted, drifted, day by day,
   Pilotless on pathless way.
It has drifted till each plank
Is oozy as the oyster-bank:
   Drifted, drifted, night by night,
   Craft that never shows a light;
Nor ever, to prevent worse knell,
Tolls in fog the warning bell.

From collision never shrinking,
Drive what may through darksome smother;
Saturate, but never sinking,
Fatal only to the *other*!
   Deadlier than the sunken reef
Since still the snare it shifteth,
   Torpid in dumb ambuscade
Waylayingly it drifteth.

   O, the sailors—O, the sails!
   O, the lost crews never heard of!
   Well the harp of Ariel wails
   Thoughts that tongue can tell no word of!

Minor Sea Pieces

TO THE MASTER OF THE "METEOR"

Lonesome on earth's loneliest deep,
Sailor! who dost thy vigil keep—
Off the Cape of Storms dost musing sweep
Over monstrous waves that curl and comb;
Of thee we think when here from brink
We blow the mead in bubbling foam.

Of thee we think, in a ring we link;
To the shearer of ocean's fleece we drink,
And the *Meteor* rolling home.

FAR OFF-SHORE

Look, the raft, a signal flying,
  Thin—a shred;
None upon the lashed spars lying,
  Quick or dead.

Cries the sea-fowl, hovering over,
  "Crew, the crew?"
And the billow, reckless, rover,
  Sweeps anew!

THE MAN-OF-WAR HAWK

Yon black man-of-war-hawk that wheels in the light
O'er the black ship's white sky-s'l, sunned cloud to the sight,
Have we low-flyers wings to ascend to his height?

No arrow can reach him; nor thought can attain
To the placid supreme in the sweep of his reign.

THE FIGURE-HEAD

The *Charles-and-Emma* seaward sped,
(Named from the carven pair at prow,)
He so smart, and a curly head,
She tricked forth as a bride knows how:
    Pretty stem for the port, I trow!

But iron-rust and alum-spray
And chafing gear, and sun and dew
Vexed this lad and lassie gay,
Tears in their eyes, salt tears nor few;
    And the hug relaxed with the failing glue.

But came in end a dismal night,
With creaking beams and ribs that groan,
A black lee-shore and waters white:
Dropped on the reef, the pair lie prone:
    O, the breakers dance, but the winds they moan!

THE GOOD CRAFT "SNOW-BIRD"

Strenuous need that head-wind be
    From purposed voyage that drives at last
The ship, sharp-braced and dogged still,
    Beating up against the blast.

Brigs that figs for market gather,
    Homeward-bound upon the stretch,
Encounter oft this uglier weather,
    Yet in end their port they fetch.

Mark yon craft from sunny Smyrna
    Glazed with ice in Boston Bay;
Out they toss the fig-drums cheerly,
    Livelier for the frosty ray.

What if sleet off-shore assailed her,
    What though ice yet plate her yards;
In wintry port not less she renders
    Summer's gift with warm regards!

And, look, the underwriters' man,
   Timely, when the stevedore's done,
Puts on his *specs* to pry and scan,
   And sets her down—*A, No. 1.*

Bravo, master! Brava, brig!
   For slanting snows out of the West
Never the *Snow-Bird* cares one fig;
   And foul winds steady her, though a pest.

OLD COUNSEL
OF THE YOUNG MASTER OF A WRECKED CALIFORNIA CLIPPER

Come out of the Golden Gate,
Go round the Horn with streamers,
Carry royals early and late;
But, brother, be not over-elate—
All hands save ship! has startled dreamers.

THE TUFT OF KELP

All dripping in tangles green,
   Cast up by a lonely sea
If purer for that, O Weed,
   Bitterer, too, are ye?

THE MALDIVE SHARK

About the Shark, phlegmatical one,
Pale sot of the Maldive sea,
The sleek little pilot-fish, azure and slim,
How alert in attendance be.
From his saw-pit of mouth, from his charnel of maw
They have nothing of harm to dread,

But liquidly glide on his ghastly flank
Or before his Gorgonian head;
Or lurk in the port of serrated teeth
In white triple tiers of glittering gates,
And there find a haven when peril's abroad,
An asylum in jaws of the Fates!
They are friends; and friendly they guide him to prey,
Yet never partake of the treat—
Eyes and brains to the dotard lethargic and dull,
Pale ravener of horrible meat.

TO NED

Where is the world we roved, Ned Bunn?
   Hollows thereof lay rich in shade
By voyagers old inviolate thrown
   Ere Paul Pry cruised with Pelf and Trade.
To us old lads some thoughts come home
Who roamed a world young lads no more shall roam.

Nor less the satiate year impends
   When, wearying of routine-resorts,
The pleasure-hunter shall break loose,
   Ned, for our Pantheistic ports:—
Marquesas and glenned isles that be
Authentic Edens in a Pagan sea.

The charm of scenes untried shall lure,
   And, Ned, a legend urge the flight—
The Typee-truants under stars
   Unknown to Shakespere's *Midsummer-Night;*
And man, if lost to Saturn's Age,
Yet feeling life no Syrian pilgrimage.

But, tell, shall he, the tourist, find
   Our isles the same in violet-glow
Enamoring us what years and years—
   Ah, Ned, what years and years ago!

Well, Adam advances, smart in pace,
But scarce by violets that advance you trace.

But we, in anchor-watches calm,
   The Indian Psyche's languor won,
And, musing, breathed primeval balm
   From Edens ere yet overrun;
Marvelling mild if mortal twice,
Here and hereafter, touch a Paradise.

CROSSING THE TROPICS
(FROM *"The Saya-Y-Manto."*)

While now the Pole Star sinks from sight
   The Southern Cross it climbs the sky;
But losing thee, my love, my light,
O bride but for one bridal night,
   The loss no rising joys supply.

Love, love, the Trade Winds urge abaft,
And thee, from thee, they steadfast waft.

By day the blue and silver sea
   And chime of waters blandly fanned—
Nor these, nor Gama's stars to me
May yield delight since still for thee
   I long as Gama longed for land.

I yearn, I yearn, reverting turn,
My heart it streams in wake astern.
When, cut by slanting sleet, we swoop
   Where raves the world's inverted year,
If roses all your porch shall loop,
Not less your heart for me will droop
   Doubling the world's last outpost drear.

O love, O love, these oceans vast:
Love, love, it is as death were past!

THE BERG
(A DREAM)

I saw a ship of martial build
(Her standards set, her brave apparel on)
Directed as by madness mere
Against a stolid iceberg steer,
Nor budge it, though the infatuate ship went down.
The impact made huge ice-cubes fall
Sullen, in tons that crashed the deck;
But that one avalanche was all—
No other movement save the foundering wreck.

Along the spurs of ridges pale,
Not any slenderest shaft and frail,
A prism over glass-green gorges lone,
Toppled; or lace of traceries fine,
Nor pendant drops in grot or mine
Were jarred, when the stunned ship went down.
Nor sole the gulls in cloud that wheeled
Circling one snow-flanked peak afar,
But nearer fowl the floes that skimmed
And crystal beaches, felt no jar.
No thrill transmitted stirred the lock
Of jack-straw needle-ice at base;
Towers undermined by waves—the block
Atilt impending—kept their place.
Seals, dozing sleek on sliddery ledges
Slipt never, when by loftier edges
Through very inertia overthrown,
The impetuous ship in bafflement went down.

Hard Berg (methought), so cold, so vast,
With mortal damps self-overcast;
Exhaling still thy dankish breath—
Adrift dissolving, bound for death;
Though lumpish thou, a lumbering one—
A lumbering lubbard loitering slow,
Impingers rue thee and go down,
Sounding thy precipice below,
Nor stir the slimy slug that sprawls
Along thy dead indifference of walls.

THE ENVIABLE ISLES
(FROM *"Rammon."*)

Through storms you reach them and from storms are free.
    Afar descried, the foremost drear in hue,
But, nearer, green; and, on the marge, the sea
    Makes thunder low and mist of rainbowed dew.

But, inland, where the sleep that folds the hills
A dreamier sleep, the trance of God, instills—
    On uplands hazed, in wandering airs aswoon,
Slow-swaying palms salute love's cypress tree
    Adown in vale where pebbly runlets croon
A song to lull all sorrow and all glee.

Sweet-fern and moss in many a glade are here,
    Where, strown in flocks, what cheek-flushed myriads lie
Dimpling in dream—unconscious slumberers mere,
    While billows endless round the beaches die.

PEBBLES

I

Though the Clerk of the Weather insist,
    And lay down the weather-law,
Pintado and gannet they wist
That the winds blow whither they list
    In tempest or flaw.

II

Old are the creeds, but stale the schools,
    Revamped as the mode may veer,
But Orm from the schools to the beaches strays,
And, finding a Conch hoar with time, he delays
    And reverent lifts it to ear.
That Voice, pitched in far monotone,
    Shall it swerve? Shall it deviate ever?
The Seas have inspired it, and Truth—
    Truth, varying from sameness never.

III

In hollows of the liquid hills
  Where the long Blue Ridges run,
The flattery of no echo thrills,
  For echo the seas have none;
Nor aught that gives man back man's strain—
The hope of his heart, the dream in his brain.

IV

On ocean where the embattled fleets repair,
Man, suffering inflictor, sails on sufferance there.

V

Implacable I, the old implacable Sea:
  Implacable most when most I smile serene—
Pleased, not appeased, by myriad wrecks in me.

VI

Curled in the comb of yon billow Andean,
  Is it the Dragon's heaven-challenging crest?
Elemental mad ramping of ravening waters—
  Yet Christ on the Mount, and the dove in her nest!

VII

Healed of my hurt, I laud the inhuman Sea—
Yea, bless the Angels Four that there convene;
For healed I am even by their pitiless breath
Distilled in wholesome dew named rosmarine.

END

TIMOLEON
ETC.

TIMOLEON
(394 B.C.)

I

If more than once, as annals tell,
  Through blood without compunction spilt,
An egotist arch rule has snatched
And stamped the seizure with his sabre's hilt,
  And, legalized by lawyers, stood;
Shall the good heart whose patriot fire
Leaps to a deed of startling note,
Do it, then flinch? Shall good in weak expire?
  Needs goodness lack the evil grit
That stares down censorship and ban,
And dumfounds saintlier ones with this—
God's will avouched in each successful man?
  Or, put it, where dread stress inspires
A virtue beyond man's standard rate,
Seems virtue there a strain forbid—
Transcendence such as shares transgression's fate?
  If so, and wan eclipse ensue,
Yet glory await emergence won,
Is that high Providence, or Chance?
And proved it which with thee, Timoleon?
  O, crowned with laurel twined with thorn,
Not rash thy life's cross-tide I stem,
But reck the problem rolled in pang
And reach and dare to touch thy garment's hem.

II

  When Argos and Cleone strove
Against free Corinth's claim or right,
Two brothers battled for her well:
A footman one, and one a mounted knight.
  Apart in place, each braved the brunt
Till the rash cavalryman, alone,
Was wrecked against the enemy's files,
His bayard crippled and he maimed and thrown.
  Timoleon, at Timophanes' need,

Makes for the rescue through the fray,
Covers him with his shield, and takes
The darts and furious odds and fights at bay;
   Till, wrought to palor of passion dumb,
Stark terrors of death around he throws,
Warding his brother from the field
Spite failing friends dispersed and rallying foes.
   Here might he rest, in claim rest here,
Rest, and a Phidian form remain;
But life halts never, life must on,
And take with term prolonged some scar or stain.
   Yes, life must on. And latent germs
Time's seasons wake in mead and man;
And brothers, playfellows in youth,
Develop into variance wide in span.

III

   Timophanes was his mother's pride—
Her pride, her pet, even all to her
Who slackly on Timoleon looked:
her pride, her pet, even all to her
Scarce he (she mused) may proud affection stir.
   He saved my darling, gossips tell:
If so, 'twas service, yea, and fair;
But instinct ruled and duty bade,
In service such, a henchman e'en might share.
   When boys they were I helped the bent;
I made the junior feel his place,
Subserve the senior, love him, too;
And sooth he does, and that's his saving grace.
   But me the meek one never can serve,
Not he, he lacks the quality keen
To make the mother through the son
An envied dame of power, a social queen.
   But thou, my first-born, thou art I
In sex translated; joyed, I scan
My features, mine, expressed in thee;
Thou art what I would be were I a man.
   My brave Timophanes, 'tis thou
Who yet the world's fore-front shalt win,

For thine the urgent resolute way,
Self pushing panoplied self through thick and thin.
   Nor here maternal insight erred:
Foresworn, with heart that did not wince
At slaying men who kept their vows,
Her darling strides to power, and reigns—a Prince.

IV

   Because of just heart and humane,
Profound the hate Timoleon knew
For crimes of pride and men-of-prey
And impious deeds that perjurous upstarts do;
   And Corinth loved he, and in way
Old Scotia's clansman loved his clan,
Devotion one with ties how dear
And passion that late to make the rescue ran.
   But crime and kin—the terrorized town,
The silent, acquiescent mother—
Revulsion racks the filial heart,
The loyal son, the patriot true, the brother.
   In evil visions of the night
He sees the lictors of the gods,
Giant ministers of righteousness,
Their *fasces* threatened by the Furies' rods.
   But undeterred he wills to act,
Resolved thereon though Ate rise;
He heeds the voice whose mandate calls,
Or seems to call, peremptory from the skies.

V

   Nor less but by approaches mild,
And trying each prudential art,
The just one first advances him
In parley with a flushed intemperate heart.
   The brother first he seeks—alone,
And pleads; but is with laughter met;
Then comes he, in accord with two,
And these adjure the tyrant and beset;
   Whose merriment gives place to rage:
"Go," stamping, "what to me is Right?"

I am the Wrong, and lo, I reign,
And testily intolerant too in might:"
   And glooms on his mute brother pale,
Who goes aside; with muffled face
He sobs the predetermined word,
And Right in Corinth reassumes its place.

VI

   But on his robe, ah, whose the blood?
And craven ones their eyes avert,
And heavy is a mother's ban,
And dismal faces of the fools can hurt.
   The whispering-gallery of the world,
Where each breathed slur runs wheeling wide
Eddies a false perverted truth,
Inveterate turning still on fratricide.
   The time was Plato's. Wandering lights
Confirmed the atheist's standing star;
As now, no sanction Virtue knew
For deeds that on prescriptive morals jar.
   Reaction took misgiving's tone,
Infecting conscience, till betrayed
To doubt the irrevocable doom
Herself had authorized when undismayed.
   Within perturbed Timoleon here
Such deeps were bared as when the sea
Convulsed, vacates its shoreward bed,
And Nature's last reserves show nakedly.
   He falters, and from Hades' glens
By night insidious tones implore—
Why suffer? hither come and be
What Phocion is who feeleth man no more.
   But, won from that, his mood elects
To live—to live in wilding place;
For years self-outcast, he but meets
In shades his playfellow's reproachful face.
   Estranged through one transcendent deed
From common membership in mart,
In severance he is like a head
Pale after battle trunkless found apart.

VII

But flood-tide comes though long the ebb,
Nor patience bides with passion long;
Like sightless orbs his thoughts are rolled
Arraigning heaven as compromised in wrong:
    To second causes why appeal?
Vain parleying here with fellow clods.
To you, Arch Principals, I rear
My quarrel, for this quarrel is with gods.
    Shall just men long to quit your world?
It is aspersion of your reign;
Your marbles in the temple stand—
Yourselves as stony and invoked in vain?
    Ah, bear with one quite overborne,
Olympians, if he chide ye now;
Magnanimous be even though he rail
And hard against ye set the bleaching brow.
    If conscience doubt, she'll next recant.
What basis then? O, tell at last,
Are earnest natures staggering here
But fatherless shadows from no substance cast?
    Yea, *are* ye, gods? Then ye, 'tis ye
Should show what touch of tie ye may,
Since ye, too, if not wrung are wronged
By grievous misconceptions of your sway.
    But deign, some little sign be given—
Low thunder in your tranquil skies;
Me reassure, nor let me be
Like a lone dog that for a master cries.

VIII

Men's moods, as frames, must yield to years,
And turns the world in fickle ways;
Corinth recalls Timoleon—ay,
And plumes him forth, but yet with schooling phrase.
    On Sicily's fields, through arduous wars,
A peace he won whose rainbow spanned
The isle redeemed; and he was hailed
Deliverer of that fair colonial land.
    And Corinth clapt: Absolved, and more!

Justice in long arrears is thine:
Not slayer of thy brother, no,
But savior of the state, Jove's soldier, man divine.
  Eager for thee thy City waits:
Return! with bays we dress your door.
But he, the Isle's loved guest, reposed,
And never for Corinth left the adopted shore.

AFTER THE PLEASURE PARTY
LINES TRACED UNDER AN IMAGE OF AMOR THREATENING

Fear me, virgin whosoever
Taking pride from love exempt,
  Fear me, slighted. Never, never
Brave me, nor my fury tempt:
Downy wings, but wroth they beat
Tempest even in reason's seat.

Behind the house the upland falls
With many an odorous tree—
White marbles gleaming through green halls,
Terrace by terrace, down and down,
And meets the starlit Mediterranean Sea.

  'Tis Paradise. In such an hour
Some pangs that rend might take release.
Nor less perturbed who keeps this bower
Of balm, nor finds balsamic peace?
From whom the passionate words in vent
After long revery's discontent?

  Tired of the homeless deep,
Look how their flight yon hurrying billows urge,
Hitherward but to reap
Passive repulse from the iron-bound verge!
Insensate, can they never know
'Tis mad to wreck the impulsion so?

An art of memory is, they tell:
But to forget! forget the glade
Wherein Fate sprung Love's ambuscade,
To flout pale years of cloistral life
And flush me in this sensuous strife.
'Tis Vesta struck with Sappho's smart.
No fable her delirious leap:
With more of cause in desperate heart,
Myself could take it—but to sleep!

Now first I feel, what all may ween,
That soon or late, if faded e'en,
One's sex asserts itself. Desire,
The dear desire through love to sway,
Is like the Geysers that aspire—
Through cold obstruction win their fervid way.
But baffled here—to take disdain,
To feel rule's instinct, yet not reign;
To dote, to come to this drear shame—
Hence the winged blaze that sweeps my soul
Like prairie fires that spurn control,
Where withering weeds incense the flame.

And kept I long heaven's watch for this,
Contemning love, for this, even this?
O terrace chill in Northern air,
O reaching ranging tube I placed
Against yon skies, and fable chased
Till, fool, I hailed for sister there
Starred Cassiopea in Golden Chair.
In dream I throned me, nor I saw
In cell the idiot crowned with straw.

And yet, ah yet scarce ill I reigned,
Through self-illusion self-sustained,
When now—enlightened, undeceived—
What gain I barrenly bereaved!
Than this can be yet lower decline—
Envy and spleen, can these be mine?

The peasant girl demure that trod
Beside our wheels that climbed the way,

And bore along a blossoming rod
That looked the sceptre of May-day—
On her—to fire this petty hell,
His softened glance how moistly fell!
The cheat! on briars her buds were strung;
And wiles peeped forth from mien how meek.
The innocent bare-foot! young, so young!
To girls, strong man's a novice weak.
To tell such beads! And more remain,
Sad rosary of belittling pain.

When after lunch and sallies gay,
Like the Decameron folk we lay
In sylvan groups; and I—let be!
O, dreams he, can he dream that one
Because not roseate feels no sun?
The plain lone bramble thrills with Spring
As much as vines that grapes shall bring.

Me now fair studies charm no more.
Shall great thoughts writ, or high themes sung
Damask wan cheeks—unlock his arm
About some radiant ninny flung?
How glad with all my starry lore,
I'd buy the veriest wanton's rose
Would but my bee therein repose.

Could I remake me! or set free
This sexless bound in sex, then plunge
Deeper than Sappho, in a lunge
Piercing Pan's paramount mystery!
For, Nature, in no shallow surge
Against thee either sex may urge,
Why hast thou made us but in halves—
Co-relatives? This makes us slaves.
If these co-relatives never meet
Self-hood itself seems incomplete.
And such the dicing of blind fate
Few matching halves here meet and mate.
What Cosmic jest or Anarch blunder
The human integral clove asunder
And shied the fractions through life's gate?

Ye stars that long your votary knew
Rapt in her vigil, see me here!
Whither is gone the spell ye threw
When rose before me Cassiopea?
Usurped on by love's stronger reign—
But lo, your very selves do wane:
Light breaks—truth breaks! Silvered no more,
But chilled by dawn that brings the gale
Shivers yon bramble above the vale,
And disillusion opens all the shore.

One knows not if Urania yet
The pleasure-party may forget;
Or whether she lived down the strain
Of turbulent heart and rebel brain;
For Amor so resents a slight,
And hers had been such haught disdain,
He long may wreak his boyish spite,
And boy-like, little reck the pain.

One knows not, no. But late in Rome
(For queens discrowned a congruous home)
Entering Albani's porch she stood
Fixed by an antique pagan stone
Colossal carved. No anchorite seer,
Not Thomas a Kempis, monk austere,
Religious more are in their tone;
Yet far, how far from Christian heart
That form august of heathen Art.
Swayed by its influence, long she stood,
Till surged emotion seething down,
She rallied and this mood she won:

Languid in frame for me,
To-day by Mary's convent shrine,
Touched by her picture's moving plea
In that poor nerveless hour of mine,
I mused—A wanderer still must grieve.
Half I resolved to kneel and believe,
Believe and submit, the veil take on.
But thee, armed Virgin! less benign,
Thee now I invoke, thou mightier one.

Helmeted woman—if such term
Befit thee, far from strife
Of that which makes the sexual feud
And clogs the aspirant life—
O self-reliant, strong and free,
Thou in whom power and peace unite,
Transcender! raise me up to thee,
Raise me and arm me!

                              Fond appeal.
For never passion peace shall bring,
Nor Art inanimate for long
Inspire. Nothing may help or heal
While Amor incensed remembers wrong.
Vindictive, not himself he'll spare;
For scope to give his vengeance play
Himself he'll blaspheme and betray.

   Then for Urania, virgins everywhere,
O pray! Example take too, and have care.

THE NIGHT-MARCH

With banners furled, and clarions mute,
   An army passes in the night;
And beaming spears and helms salute
   The dark with bright.

In silence deep the legions stream,
   With open ranks, in order true;
Over boundless plains they stream and gleam—
   No chief in view!

Afar, in twinkling distance lost,
   (So legends tell) he lonely wends
And back through all that shining host
   His mandate sends.

THE RAVAGED VILLA

In shards the sylvan vases lie,
  Their links of dance undone,
And brambles wither by thy brim,
  Choked fountain of the sun!
The spider in the laurel spins,
  The weed exiles the flower:
And, flung to kiln, Apollo's bust
  Makes lime for Mammon's tower.

THE MARGRAVE'S BIRTHNIGHT

Up from many a sheeted valley,
From white woods as well,
Down too from each fleecy upland
Jingles many a bell

Jovial on the work-sad horses
Hitched to runners old
Of the toil-worn peasants sledging
Under sheepskins in the cold;

Till from every quarter gathered
Meet they on one ledge,
There from hoods they brush the snow off
Lighting from each sledge

Full before the Margrave's castle,
Summoned there to cheer
On his birth-night, in mid-winter,
Kept year after year.

O the hall, and O the holly!
Tables line each wall;
Guests as holly-berries plenty,
But—no host withal!

May his people feast contented
While at head of board
Empty throne and vacant cover
Speak the absent lord?

Minstrels enter. And the stewards
Serve the guests; and when,
Passing there the vacant cover,
Functionally then

Old observance grave they offer;
But no Margrave fair,
In his living aspect gracious,
Sits responsive there;

No, and never guest once marvels,
None the good lord name,
Scarce they mark void throne and cover—
Dust upon the same.

Mindless as to what importeth
Absence such in hall;
Tacit as the plough-horse feeding
In the palfrey's stall.

Ah, enough for toil and travail,
If but for a night
Into wine is turned the water,
Black bread into white.

MAGIAN WINE

Amulets gemmed, to Miriam dear,
  Adown in liquid mirage gleam;
Solomon's Syrian charms appear,
  Opal and ring supreme.
The rays that light this Magian Wine
Thrill up from semblances divine.

And, seething through the rapturous wave,
What low Elysian anthems rise:
Sibylline inklings blending rave,
 Then lap the verge with sighs.
Delirious here the oracles swim
Ambiguous in the beading hymn.

THE GARDEN OF METRODORUS

The Athenians mark the moss-grown gate
And hedge untrimmed that hides the haven green:
 And who keeps here his quiet state?
 And shares he sad or happy fate
Where never foot-path to the gate is seen?

Here none come forth, here none go in,
Here silence strange, and dumb seclusion dwell:
 Content from loneness who may win?
 And is this stillness peace or sin
Which noteless thus apart can keep its dell?

THE NEW ZEALOT TO THE SUN

 Persian, you rise
Aflame from climes of sacrifice
 Where adulators sue,
And prostrate man, with brow abased,
Adheres to rites whose tenor traced
 All worship hitherto.

 Arch type of sway,
Meetly your over-ruling ray
 You fling from Asia's plain,
Whence flashed the javelins abroad
Of many a wild incursive horde
 Led by some shepherd Cain.

Mid terrors dinned
Gods too came conquerors from your Ind,
    The brood of Brahma throve;
They came like to the scythed car,
Westward they rolled their empire far,
    Of night their purple wove.

Chemist, you breed
In orient climes each sorcerous weed
    That energizes dream—
Transmitted, spread in myths and creeds,
Houris and hells, delirious screeds
    And Calvin's last extreme.

What though your light
In time's first dawn compelled the flight
    Of Chaos' startled clan,
Shall never all your darted spears
Disperse worse Anarchs, frauds and fears,
    Sprung from these weeds to man?

But Science yet
An effluence ampler shall beget,
    And power beyond your play—
Shall quell the shades you fail to rout,
Yea, searching every secret out
    Elucidate your ray.

THE WEAVER

For years within a mud-built room
For Arva's shrine he weaves the shawl,
Lone wight, and at a lonely loom,
His busy shadow on the wall.

The face is pinched, the form is bent,
No pastime knows he nor the wine,
Recluse he lives and abstinent
Who weaves for Arva's shrine.

LAMIA'S SONG

Descent, descend!
   Pleasant the downward way—
From your lonely Alp
With the wintry scalp
To our myrtles in valleys of May.
   Wend then, wend:
Mountaineer, descend!
And more than a wreath shall repay.
   Come, ah come!
With the cataracts come,
That hymn as they roam
How pleasant the downward way!

IN A GARRET

Gems and jewels let them heap—
 Wax sumptuous as the Sophi:
For me, to grapple from Art's deep
 One dripping trophy!

MONODY

To have known him, to have loved him
 After loneness long;
And then to be estranged in life,
 And neither in the wrong;
And now for death to set his seal—
 Ease me, a little ease, my song!

By wintry hills his hermit-mound
 The sheeted snow-drifts drape,
And houseless there the snow-bird flits
 Beneath the fir-trees' crape:
Glazed now with ice the cloistral vine
 That hid the shyest grape.

LONE FOUNTS

Though fast youth's glorious fable flies,
View not the world with worlding's eyes;
Nor turn with weather of the time.
Foreclose the coming of surprise:
Stand where Posterity shall stand;
Stand where the Ancients stood before,
And, dipping in lone founts thy hand,
Drink of the never-varying lore:
Wise once, and wise thence evermore.

THE BENCH OF BOORS

In bed I muse on Tenier's boors,
Embrowned and beery losels all:
    A wakeful brain
    Elaborates pain:
Within low doors the slugs of boors
Laze and yawn and doze again.

In dreams they doze, the drowsy boors,
Their hazy hovel warm and small:
    Thought's ampler bound
    But chill is found:
Within low doors the basking boors
Snugly hug the ember-mound.

Sleepless, I see the slumberous boors
Their blurred eyes blink, their eyelids fall:
    Thought's eager sight
    Aches—overbright!
Within low doors the boozy boors
Cat-naps take in pipe-bowl light.

THE ENTHUSIAST
"THOUGH HE SLAY ME YET WILL I TRUST IN HIM."

Shall hearts that beat no base retreat
  In youth's magnanimous years—
Ignoble hold it, if discreet
  When interest tames to fears;
Shall spirits that worship light
  Perfidious deem its sacred glow,
  Recant, and trudge where worldlings go,
Conform and own them right?

Shall Time with creeping influence cold
  Unnerve and cow? the heart
Pine for the heartless ones enrolled
  With palterers of the mart?
Shall faith abjure her skies,
  Or pale probation blench her down
  To shrink from Truth so still, so lone
Mid loud gregarious lies?

Each burning boat in Caesar's rear,
  Flames—No return through me!
So put the torch to ties though dear,
  If ties but tempters be.
Nor cringe if come the night:
  Walk through the cloud to meet the pall,
  Though light forsake thee, never fall
From fealty to light.

ART

In placid hours well-pleased we dream
Of many a brave unbodied scheme.
But form to lend, pulsed life create,
What unlike things must meet and mate:
A flame to melt—a wind to freeze;
Sad patience—joyous energies;

Humility—yet pride and scorn;
Instinct and study; love and hate;
Audacity—reverence. These must mate,
And fuse with Jacob's mystic heart,
To wrestle with the angel—Art.

BUDDHA

"FOR WHAT IS YOUR LIFE? IT IS EVEN A VAPOR THAT APPEARETH FOR A LITTLE TIME AND THEN VANISHETH AWAY."

Swooning swim to less and less,
    Aspirant to nothingness!
Sobs of the worlds, and dole of kinds
    That dumb endurers be—
Nirvana! absorb us in your skies,
    Annul us into thee.

C——'S LAMENT

How lovely was the light of heaven,
What angels leaned from out the sky
In years when youth was more than wine
And man and nature seemed divine
Ere yet I felt that youth must die.

Ere yet I felt that youth must die
How insubstantial looked the earth,
Alladin-land! in each advance,
Or here or there, a new romance;
I never dreamed would come a dearth.

And nothing then but had its worth,
Even pain. Yes, pleasure still and pain
In quick reaction made of life
A lovers' quarrel, happy strife
In youth that never comes again.

But will youth never come again?
Even to his grave-bed has he gone,
And left me lone to wake by night
With heavy heart that erst was light?
O, lay it at his head—a stone!

SHELLEY'S VISION

Wandering late by morning seas
When my heart with pain was low—
Hate the censor pelted me—
Deject I saw my shadow go.

In elf-caprice of bitter tone
I too would pelt the pelted one:
At my shadow I cast a stone.

When lo, upon that sun-lit ground
I saw the quivering phantom take
The likeness of St. Stephen crowned:
Then did self-reverence awake.

FRAGMENTS OF A LOST GNOSTIC POEM OF THE 12TH CENTURY

*   *   *   *

Found a family, build a state,
The pledged event is still the same:
Matter in end will never abate
His ancient brutal claim.

*   *   *   *

Indolence is heaven's ally here,
And energy the child of hell:
The Good Man pouring from his pitcher clear,
But brims the poisoned well.

THE MARCHIONESS OF BRINVILLIERS

He toned the sprightly beam of morning
   With twilight meek of tender eve,
Brightness interfused with softness,
   Light and shade did weave:
And gave to candor equal place
With mystery starred in open skies;
And, floating all in sweetness, made
   Her fathomless mild eyes.

THE AGE OF THE ANTONINES

While faith forecasts millennial years
   Spite Europe's embattled lines,
Back to the Past one glance be cast—
   The Age of the Antonines!
O summit of fate, O zenith of time
When a pagan gentleman reigned,
And the olive was nailed to the inn of the world
Nor the peace of the just was feigned.
   A halcyon Age, afar it shines,
Solstice of Man and the Antonines.

Hymns to the nations' friendly gods
Went up from the fellowly shrines,
No demagogue beat the pulpit-drum
   In the Age of the Antonines!
The sting was not dreamed to be taken from death,
No Paradise pledged or sought,
But they reasoned of fate at the flowing feast,
Nor stifled the fluent thought.
   We sham, we shuffle while faith declines—
They were frank in the Age of the Antonines.

Orders and ranks they kept degree,
Few felt how the parvenu pines,
No law-maker took the lawless one's fee
   In the Age of the Antonines!

Under law made will the world reposed
And the ruler's right confessed,
For the heavens elected the Emperor then,
The foremost of men the best.
    Ah, might we read in America's signs
The Age restored of the Antonines.

HERBA SANTA

I

After long wars when comes release
Not olive wands proclaiming peace
    An import dearer share
Than stems of Herba Santa hazed
    In autumn's Indian air.
Of moods they breathe that care disarm,
They pledge us lenitive and calm.

II

Shall code or creed a lure afford
To win all selves to Love's accord?
When Love ordained a supper divine
    For the wide world of man,
What bickerings o'er his gracious wine!
    Then strange new feuds began.

Effectual more in lowlier way,
    Pacific Herb, thy sensuous plea
The bristling clans of Adam sway
    At least to fellowship in thee!
Before thine altar tribal flags are furled,
Fain woulds't thou make one hearthstone of the world.

III

To scythe, to sceptre, pen and hod—
    Yea, sodden laborers dumb;
To brains overplied, to feet that plod,

In solace of the *Truce of God*
   The Calumet has come!

IV

Ah for the world ere Raleigh's find
   Never that knew this suasive balm
That helps when Gilead's fails to heal,
   Helps by an interserted charm.

Insinuous thou that through the nerve
   Windest the soul, and so canst win
   Some from repinings, some from sin,
The Church's aim thou dost subserve.

The ruffled fag fordone with care
   And brooding, Gold would ease this pain:
Him soothest thou and smoothest down
Till some content return again.

Even ruffians feel thy influence breed
   Saint Martin's summer in the mind,
They feel this last evangel plead,
As did the first, apart from creed,
   Be peaceful, man—be kind!

V

Rejected once on higher plain,
O Love supreme, to come again
   Can this be thine?
Again to come, and win us too
   In likeness of a weed
That as a god didst vainly woo,
   As man more vainly bleed?

VI

Forbear, my soul! and in thine Eastern chamber
   Rehearse the dream that brings the long release:
Through jasmine sweet and talismanic amber
   Inhaling Herba Santa in the passive Pipe of Peace.

FRUIT OF TRAVEL LONG AGO

VENICE

With Pantheist energy of will
The little craftsman of the Coral Sea
Strenuous in the blue abyss,
Up-builds his marvelous gallery
   And long arcade,
Erections freaked with many a fringe
   Of marble garlandry,
Evincing what a worm can do.

Laborious in a shallower wave,
   Advanced in kindred art,
A prouder agent proved Pan's might
When Venice rose in reefs of palaces.

IN A BYE-CANAL

A swoon of noon, a trance of tide,
The hushed siesta brooding wide
   Like calms far off Peru;
No floating wayfarer in sight,
Dumb noon, and haunted like the night
   When Jael the wiled one slew.
A languid impulse from the oar
Plied by my indolent gondolier
Tinkles against a palace hoar,
   And, hark, response I hear!
A lattice clicks; and lo, I see
Between the slats, mute summoning me,
What loveliest eyes of scintillation,
What basilisk glance of conjuration!

   Fronted I have, part taken the span
Of portents in nature and peril in man.
I have swum—I have been
Twixt the whale's black flukes and the white shark's fin;
The enemy's desert have wandered in,

And there have turned, have turned and scanned,
Following me how noiselessly,
Envy and Slander, lepers hand in hand.
All this. But at the latticed eye—
"Hey! Gondolier, you sleep, my man;
Wake up!" And, shooting by, we ran;
The while I mused, This, surely now,
Confutes the Naturalists, allow!
Sirens, true sirens verily be,
Sirens, waylayers in the sea.

Well, wooed by these same deadly misses,
Is it shame to run?
No! flee them did divine Ulysses,
   Brave, wise, and Venus' son.

PISA'S LEANING TOWER

The Tower in tiers of architraves,
Fair circle over cirque,
A trunk of rounded colonades,
The maker's master-work,
Impends with all its pillared tribes,
And, poising them, debates:
It thinks to plunge—but hesitates;
Shrinks back—yet fain would slide;
Withholds itself—itself would urge;
Hovering, shivering on the verge,
   A would-be suicide!

IN A CHURCH OF PADUA

In vaulted place where shadows flit,
An upright sombre box you see:
A door, but fast, and lattice none,
But punctured holes minutely small

In lateral silver panel square
Above a kneeling-board without,
Suggest an aim if not declare.

Who bendeth here the tremulous knee
No glimpse may get of him within,
And he immured may hardly see
The soul confessing there the sin;
Nor yields the low-sieved voice a tone
Whereby the murmurer may be known.

Dread diving-bell! In thee inurned
What hollows the priest must sound,
Descending into consciences
　　Where more is hid than found.

MILAN CATHEDRAL

Through light green haze, a rolling sea
　　Over gardens where redundance flows,
　　The fat old plain of Lombardy,
The White Cathedral shows.

　　Of Art the miracles
　　Its tribes of pinnacles
Gleam like to ice-peaks snowed; and higher,
Erect upon each airy spire
　　In concourse without end,
Statues of saints over saints ascend
Like multitudinous forks of fire.

What motive was the master-builder's here?
Why these synodic hierarchies given,
Sublimely ranked in marble sessions clear,
Except to signify the host of heaven.

PAUSILIPPO
(IN THE TIME OF BOMBA)

A hill there is that laves its feet
In Naples' bay and lifts its head
In jovial season, curled with vines.
Its name, in pristine years conferred
By settling Greeks, imports that none
Who take the prospect thence can pine,
For such the charm of beauty shown
Even sorrow's self they cheerful weened
Surcease might find and thank good Pan.

    Toward that hill my landeau drew;
And there, hard by the verge, was seen
Two faces with such meaning fraught
One scarce could mark and straight pass on.

    A man it was less hoar with time
Than bleached through strange immurement long,
Retaining still, by doom depressed,
Dim trace of some aspiring prime.
Seated he tuned a homely harp
Watched by a girl, whose filial mien
Toward one almost a child again,
Took on a staid maternal tone.
Nor might one question that the locks
Which in smoothed natural silvery curls
Fell on the bowed one's thread-bare coat
Betrayed her ministering hand.

    Anon, among some ramblers drawn,
A murmur rose "Tis Silvio, Silvio!"
With inklings more in tone suppressed
Touching his story, part recalled:
Clandestine arrest abrupt by night;
The sole conjecturable cause
The yearning in a patriot ode
Construed as treason; trial none;
Prolonged captivity profound;
Vain liberation late. All this,

With pity for impoverishment
And blight forestalling age's wane.

  Hillward the quelled enthusiast turned,
Unmanned, made meek through strenuous wrong,
Preluding, faltering; then began,
But only thrilled the wire—no more,
The constant maid supplying voice,
Hinting by no ineloquent sign
That she was but his mouth-piece mere,
Himself too spiritless and spent.

    Pausilippo, Pausilippo,
Pledging easement unto pain,
    Shall your beauty even solace
If one's sense of beauty wane?

Could light airs that round ye play
Waft heart-heaviness away
Or memory lull to sleep,
    Then, then indeed your balm
    Might Silvio becharm,
And life in fount would leap,
    Pausilippo!

Did not your spell invite,
    In moods that slip between,
    A dream of years serene,
And wake, to dash, delight—
    Evoking here in vision
    Fulfilment and fruition—
Nor mine, nor meant for man!
    Did hope not frequent share
    The mirage when despair
Overtakes the caravan,
    Me then your scene might move
    To break from sorrow's snare,
    And apt your name would prove,
    Pausilippo!

But I've looked upon your revel—
    It unravels not the pain:

Pausilippo, Pausilippo,
  Named benignly if in vain!

  It ceased. In low and languid tone
The tideless ripple lapped the passive shore;
As listlessly the bland untroubled heaven
Looked down as silver doled was silent given
In pity—futile as the ore!

THE ATTIC LANDSCAPE

Tourist, spare the avid glance
  That greedy roves the sight to see:
Little here of "Old Romance,"
  Or Picturesque of Tivoli.

No flushful tint the sense to warm—
Pure outline pale, a linear charm.
The clear-cut hills carved temples face,
Respond, and share their sculptural grace.

'Tis Art and Nature lodged together,
  Sister by sister, cheek to cheek;
Such Art, such Nature, and such weather
  The All-in-All seems here a Greek.

THE SAME

A circumambient spell it is,
  Pellucid on these scenes that waits,
Repose that does of Plato tell—
  Charm that his style authenticates.

THE PARTHENON

I
SEEN ALOFT FROM AFAR

Estranged in site,
Aerial gleaming, warmly white,
You look a suncloud motionless
In noon of day divine;
Your beauty charmed enhancement takes
In Art's long after-shine.

II
NEARER VIEWED

Like Lais, fairest of her kind,
In subtlety your form's defined—
The cornice curved, each shaft inclined,
While yet, to eyes that do but revel
    And take the sweeping view,
Erect this seems, and that a level,
    To line and plummet true.

Spinoza gazes; and in mind
Dreams that one architect designed
    Lais—and you!

III
THE FRIEZE

What happy musings genial went
With airiest touch the chisel lent
    To frisk and curvet light
Of horses gay—their riders grave—
Contrasting so in action brave
    With virgins meekly bright,
Clear filing on in even tone
With pitcher each, one after one
    Like water-fowl in flight.

IV
THE LAST TILE

When the last marble tile was laid
The winds died down on all the seas;
  Hushed were the birds, and swooned the glade;
  Ictinus sat; Aspasia said
"Hist!—Art's meridian, Pericles!"

GREEK MASONRY

Joints were none that mortar sealed:
Together, scarce with line revealed,
The blocks in symmetry congealed.

GREEK ARCHITECTURE

Not magnitude, not lavishness,
But Form—the Site;
Not innovating wilfulness,
But reverence for the Archetype.

OFF CAPE COLONNA

Aloof they crown the foreland lone,
  From aloft they loftier rise—
Fair columns, in the aureola rolled
  From sunned Greek seas and skies.
They wax, sublimed to fancy's view,
A god-like group against the blue.

Over much like gods! Serene they saw
  The wolf-waves board the deck,
And headlong hull of Falconer,
  And many a deadlier wreck.

THE ARCHIPELAGO

Sail before the morning breeze
The Sporads through and Cyclades
They look like isles of absentees—
        Gone whither?

You bless Apollo's cheering ray,
But Delos, his own isle, today
Not e'en a Selkirk there to pray
        God friend me!

Scarce lone these groups, scarce lone and bare
When Theseus roved a Raleigh there,
Each isle a small Virginia fair—
        Unravished.

Nor less through havoc fell they rue,
They still retain in outline true
Their grace of form when earth was new
        And primal.

But beauty clear, the frame's as yet,
Never shall make one quite forget
Thy picture, Pan, therein once set—
        Life's revel!

'Tis Polynesia reft of palms,
Seaward no valley breathes her balms—
Not such as musk thy rings of calms,
        Marquesas!

SYRA
(A TRANSMITTED REMINISCENCE.)

Fleeing from Scio's smouldering vines
(Where when the sword its work had done
The Turk applied the torch) the Greek
Came here, a fugitive stript of goods,
Here to an all but tenantless isle,
Nor here in footing gained at first,

Felt safe. Still from the turbaned foe
Dreading the doom of shipwrecked men
Whom feline seas permit to land
Then pounce upon and drag them back,
For height they made, and prudent won
A cone-shaped fastness on whose flanks
With pains they pitched their eyrie camp,
Stone huts, whereto they wary clung;
But, reassured in end, come down—
Multiplied through compatriots now,
Refugees like themselves forlorn—
And building along the water's verge
Begin to thrive; and thriving more
When Greece at last flung off the Turk,
Make of the haven mere a mart.

  I saw it in its earlier day—
Primitive, such an isled resort
As hearthless Homer might have known
Wandering about the Ægean here.
Sheds ribbed with wreck-stuff faced the sea
Where goods in transit shelter found;
And here and there a shanty-shop
Where Fez-caps, swords, tobacco, shawls
Pistols, and orient finery, Eve's—
(The spangles dimmed by hands profane)
Like plunder on a pirate's deck
Lay orderless in such loose way
As to suggest things ravished or gone astray.

  Above a tented inn with fluttering flag
A sunburnt board announced Greek wine
In self-same text Anacreon knew,
Dispensed by one named "Pericles."
Got up as for the opera's scene,
Armed strangers, various, lounged or lazed,
Lithe fellows tall, with gold-shot eyes.
Sunning themselves as leopards may.

  Off-shore lay xebecs trim and light,
And some but dubious in repute.
But on the strand, for docks were none,

What busy bees! no testy fry;
Frolickers, picturesquely odd,
With bales and oil-jars lading boats,
Lighters that served an anchored craft,
Each in his tasseled Phrygian cap,
Blue Eastern drawers and braided vest;
And some with features cleanly cut
As Proserpine's upon the coin.
Such chatterers all! like children gay
Who make believe to work, but play.

I saw, and how help musing too.
Here traffic's immature as yet:
Forever this juvenile fun hold out
And these light hearts? Their garb, their glee,
Alike profuse in flowing measure,
Alike inapt for serious work,
Blab of grandfather Saturn's prime
When trade was not, nor toil, nor stress,
But life was leisure, merriment, peace,
And lucre none and love was righteousness.

DISINTERMENT OF THE HERMES

What forms divine in adamant fair—
Carven demigod and god,
And hero-marbles rivalling these,
Bide under Latium's sod,
Or lost in sediment and drift
Alluvial which the Grecian rivers sift.

To dig for these, O better far
Than raking arid sands
For gold more barren meetly theirs
Sterile, with brimming hands.

THE APPARITION
(THE PARTHENON UPLIFTED ON ITS ROCK FIRST CHALLENGING THE VIEW ON THE APPROACH TO ATHENS)

Abrupt the supernatural Cross,
   Vivid in startled air,
Smote the Emperor Constantine
And turned his soul's allegiance there.

With other power appealing down,
   Trophy of Adam's best!
If cynic minds you scarce convert,
You try them, shake them, or molest.

Diogenes, that honest heart,
   Lived ere your date began;
Thee had he seen, he might have swerved
In mood nor barked so much at Man.

IN THE DESERT

Never Pharoah's Night,
Whereof the Hebrew wizards croon,
Did so the Theban flamens try
As me this veritable Noon.

Like blank ocean in blue calm
Undulates the ethereal frame;
In one flowing oriflamme
God flings his fiery standard out.

Battling with the Emirs fierce
Napoleon a great victory won,
Through and through his sword did pierce;
But, bayonetted by this sun
His gunners drop beneath the gun.

Holy, holy, holy Light!
Immaterial incandescence,
Of God the effluence of the essence,
Shekinah intolerably bright!

THE GREAT PYRAMID

Your masonry—and is it man's?
More like some Cosmic artisan's.
Your courses as in strata rise,
Beget you do a blind surmise
     Like Grampians.

Far slanting up your sweeping flank
Arabs with Alpine goats may rank,
And there they find a choice of passes
Even like to dwarfs that climb the masses
     Of glaciers blank.

Shall lichen in your crevice fit?
Nay, sterile all and granite-knit:
Weather nor weather-strain ye rue,
But aridly you cleave the blue
     As lording it.

Morn's vapor floats beneath your peak,
Kites skim your side with pinion weak;
To sand-storms battering, blow on blow,
Raging to work your overthrow,
     You—turn the cheek.

All elements unmoved you stem,
Foursquare you stand and suffer them:
Time's future infinite you dare,
While, for the past, 'tis you that wear
     Eld's diadem.

Slant from your inmost lead the caves
And labyrinths rumored. These who braves
And penetrates (old palmers said)
Comes out afar on deserts dead
     And, dying, raves.

Craftsmen, in dateless quarries dim,
Stones formless into form did trim,
Usurped on Nature's self with Art,
And bade this dumb I AM to start,
     Imposing him.

L'ENVOI
THE RETURN OF THE SIRE DE NESLE.
A.D. 16—

My towers at last! These rovings end,
Their thirst is slaked in larger dearth:
The yearning infinite recoils,
    For terrible is earth.

Kaf thrusts his snouted crags through fog:
Araxes swells beyond his span,
And knowledge poured by pilgrimage
    Overflows the banks of man.

But thou, my stay, thy lasting love
One lonely good, let this but be!
Weary to view the wide world's swarm,
    But blest to fold but thee.

ADDITIONAL POEMS

ADDITION STORMS

CAMOENS
(Before)

Forever must I fan this fire?
Forever in flame on flame aspire?
Restless, restless, craving rest—
The Imperfect toward Perfection pressed!
Yea, for the God demands thy best.
The world with endless beauty teems,
And thought evokes new worlds of dreams:
Hunt then the flying herds of themes!
And fan, yet fan thy fervid fire,
Until the crucibled gold shall show
That fire can purge, as well as glow:
In ordered ardor, nobly strong
Flame to the height of ancient song.

CAMOENS IN THE HOSPITAL
(After)

What now avails the pageant verse,
Trophies and arms with music borne?
Base is the world; and some rehearse
How noblest meet ignoble scorn.
Vain now the ardor, vain the fire,
Delirium mere, unsound desire:
Fate's knife hath ripped the chorded lyre.
Exhausted by the exacting lay,
I do but fall a surer prey
To wile and guile ill understood;
While they who work them, fair in face,
Still keep their strength in prudent place,
And claim they worthier run life's race,
Serving high God with useful good.

THE MEDALLION
IN VILLA ALBANI

Since seriousness in many a face,
Open or latent, you may trace—
The ground-expression, wherein close
All smiles at last; and ever still
The revelation of repose;
Which sums the life, and tells the mood
Of inmost self in solitude—

Then wherefore, World, of bards complain
Whose verse the years and fate imbue
With reveries where no glosings reign—
An even unelated strain
In candor grave, to nature due?

TIME'S LONG AGO!

Time's Long Ago! Nor coral isles
In the blue South Sea more serene
When the lagoons unruffled show.
There, Fates and Furies change their mien.
Though strewn with wreckage be the shore
The halcyon haunts it; all is green
And wins the heart that hope can lure no more.

IN THE HALL OF MARBLES
(LINES RECALLED FROM A DESTROYED POEM)

If genius, turned to sordid ends
    Ye count to glory lost,
How with mankind that flouts the aims
    Time's Attic years engrossed?
Waxes the world so rich and old?
    Richer and narrower, age's way?
But, primal fervors all displaced
    Our arts but serve the clay.
This plaint the sibyls unconsoled renew:
Man fell from Eden, fall from Athens too.

GOLD IN THE MOUNTAIN

Gold in the mountain
And gold in the glen,
And greed in the heart,
Heaven having no part,
And unsatisfied men.

A SPIRIT APPEARED TO ME

A Spirit appeared to me, and said
"Where now would you choose to dwell?
In the Paradise of the Fool,
Or in wise Solomon's hell?"—

Never he asked me twice:
"Give me the fool's Paradise."

MY JACKET OLD

My jacket old, with narrow seam—
When the dull day's work is done
I dust it, and of Asia dream,
Old Asia of the sun!
There other garbs prevail;
Yea, lingering there, free robe and vest
Edenic Leisure's age attest
Ere Work, alack, came in with Wail.

HEARTS-OF-GOLD

Pity, if true,
What the pewterer said—
Hearts-of-gold be few.
Howbeit, when snug in my bed,
And the fire-light flickers and yellows,
I dream of the hearts-of-gold sped—
The Falernian fellows—
Hafiz and Horace,
And Beranger—all
Dexterous tumblers eluding the Fall,
Fled? can be sped?
And the marygold's morris
Is danced o'er their head;
And their memory mellows,
Embalmed and becharmed,
Hearts-of-gold and good fellows!

PONTOOSUC

Crowning a bluff where gleams the lake below,
Some pillared pines in well-spaced order stand
And like an open temple show.
And here in best of seasons bland;
Autumnal noon-tide, I look out
From dusk arcades on sunshine all about.

Beyond the Lake, in upland cheer
Fields, pastoral fields and barns appear,
They skirt the hills where lonely roads
Revealed in links thro' tiers of woods
Wind up to indistinct abodes
And faery-peopled neighborhoods;
While further fainter mountains keep
Hazed in romance impenetrably deep.

Look, corn in stacks, on many a farm,
And orchards ripe in languorous charm,
As dreamy Nature, feeling sure
Of all her genial labor done,
And the last mellow fruitage won,
Would idle out her term mature;
Reposing like a thing reclined
In kinship with man's meditative mind.

For me, within the brown arcade—
Rich life, methought; sweet here in shade
And pleasant abroad in air!—But, nay,
A counter thought intrusive played,
A thought as old as thought itself,
And who shall lay it on the shelf!—
I felt the beauty bless the day
In opulence of autumn's dower;
But evanescence will not stay!
A year ago was such an hour,
As this, which but foreruns the blast
Shall sweep these live leaves to the dead leaves past.

All dies!—

      I stood in revery long.
Then, to forget death's ancient wrong,
I turned me in the deep arcade,
And there by chance in lateral glade
I saw low tawny mounds in lines
Relics of trunks of stately pines
Ranked erst in colonnades where, lo!
Erect succeeding pillars show!

      All dies! and not alone
The aspiring trees and men and grass;
The poet's forms of beauty pass,
And noblest deeds they are undone
Even truth itself decays, and lo,
From truth's sad ashes fraud and falsehood grow.

All dies!

The workman dies, and after him, the work;
Like to these pines whose graves I trace,
Statue and statuary fall upon their face:
In very amaranths the worm doth lurk,
Even stars, Chaldæans say, have left their place.
Andes and Apalachee tell
Of havoc ere our Adam fell,
And present Nature as a moss doth show
On the ruins of the Nature of the æons of long ago.

But look—and hark!

        Adown the glade,
Where light and shadow sport at will,
Who cometh vocal, and arrayed
As in the first pale tints of morn—
So pure, rose-clear, and fresh and chill!
Some ground-pine sprigs her brow adorn,
The earthy rootlets tangled clinging.
Over tufts of moss which dead things made,
Under vital twigs which danced or swayed,
Along she floats, and lightly singing:

"Dies, all dies!
The grass it dies, but in vernal rain
Up it springs and it lives again;
Over and over, again and again
It lives, it dies and it lives again.
Who sighs that all dies?
Summer and winter, and pleasure and pain
And everything everywhere in God's reign,
They end, and anon they begin again:
Wane and wax, wax and wane:
Over and over and over amain
End, ever end, and begin again—
End, ever end, and forever and ever begin again!"

She ceased, and nearer slid, and hung
In dewy guise; then softlier sung:

"Since light and shade are equal set
And all revolves, nor more ye know;
Ah, why should tears the pale cheek fret
For aught that waneth here below.
Let go, Let go!"

With that, her warm lips thrilled me through,
She kissed me, while her chaplet cold
Its rootlets brushed against my brow,
With all their humid clinging mould.
She vanished, leaving fragrant breath
And warmth and chill of wedded life and death.

THE ADMIRAL OF THE WHITE

Proud, O proud in his oaken hall
  The Admiral walks to-day,
From the top of his turreted citadel
  French colors 'neath English play.—

Why skips the needle so frolic about,
  Why danceth the ship so to-day?
Is it to think of those French Captains' swords
  Surrendered when ended the fray?
O well may you skip, and well may you dance,
  You dance on your homeward way;
O well may you skip and well may you dance
  With homeward-bound victors to-day.

Like a baron bold from his mountain-hold,
  At night looks the Admiral forth:
Heavy the clouds, and thick and dun,
  They slant from the sullen North.

Catching at each little opening for life,
  The moon in her wane swims forlorn;
Fades, fades mid the clouds her pinched paled face
  Like the foeman's in seas sinking down.

Tack off from the land! And the watch below
   Old England the oak-crownd to drink:—
Knock, knock, knock, the loud billows go,
   Rapping "Bravo my boys!" ere they sink—
Knock, knock, knock, on the windward bow;
   The Anvil-Head Whale you would think.

Tis Saturday night,—the last of the week,
   The last of the week, month, and year—
On deck! shout it out, you forecastle-man,
   Shout "Sail ho, Sail ho—the New Year!"

Drink, messmates, drink; 'tis sweet to think
   Tis the last of the week, month, and year,
Then perils are past, and Old England at last,
   Though now shunned, in the morn we will near;
We've beaten the foe, their ship blown below,
   Their flags in St. Paul's Church we'll rear.

Knock, knock, knock, the loud billows go—
   God! what's that shouting and roar?
Breakers!—close, close ahead and abeam:
   She strikes—knock, knock—we're ashore!

Why went the needle so trembling about,
   Why shook you, and trembled to-day?
Was it, perchance, that those French Captains' swords
   In the arm-chest too near you lay?
Was it to think that those French Captains' swords,
   Surrendered, might yet win the day?
O woe for the brave no courage can save,
   Woe, woe for the ship led astray.

High-beetling the rocks below which she shocks,
   Her boats they are stove by her side,
Fated seas lick her round, as in flames she were bound,
   Roar, roar like a furnace the tide.

O jagged the rocks, repeated she knocks,
   Splits the hull like a cracked filbert there,
Her timbers are torn, and ground-up are thrown,
   Float the small chips like filbert-bits there.

Pale, pale, but proud, 'neath the billows loud,
The Admiral sleeps tonight;
    Pale, pale, but proud, in his sea-weed shroud,—
The Admiral of the White:
    And by their gun the dutiful ones,
Who had fought, bravely fought the good fight.

THE ADMIRAL OF THE WHITE
(Copyright 1885)

By chapel bare, with walls sea-beat,
The lichened urns in wilds are lost
About a carved memorial stone
That shows, decayed and coral-mossed,
A form recumbent, swords at feet,
Trophies at head, and kelp for a winding-sheet.

I invoke thy ghost, neglected fane,
Washed by the waters' long lament;
I adjure the recumbent effigy
To tell the cenotaph's intent—
Reveal why fagotted swords are at feet,
Why trophies appear and weeds are the winding-sheet.

———————

By open ports the Admiral sits,
And shares repose with guns that tell
Of power that smote the arm'd Plate Fleet
Whose sinking flag-ship's colors fell;
But over the Admiral floats in light
His squadron's flag, the red-cross Flag of the White.

.   .   .   .

Ensigns and arms in trophy brave—
Braver for many a rent and scar,
The captor's naval hall bedeck,
Spoil that insures an earldom's star;
Toledoes great, grand draperies too,
Spain's steel and silk, and splendors from Peru.

But crippled part in splintering fight,
The vanquished flying the victor's flags,
With prize-crews, under convoy-guns,
Heavy the fleet from Opher drags—
The Admiral crowding sail ahead,
Foremost with news who foremost in conflict sped.

But out from cloistral gallery dim,
In early night his glance is thrown;
He marks the vague reserve of heaven,
He feels the touch of ocean lone;
Then turns, in frame part undermined,
Nor notes the shadowing wings that fan behind.

There, peaked and gray, three haglets fly,
And follow, follow fast in wake
Where slides the cabin-lustre shy,
And sharks from man a glamour take,
Seething along the line of light
In lane that endless rules the war-ship's flight.

.   .   .   .   .   .

But who a flattering tide may trust,
Or favoring breeze, or aught in end?—
Careening under startling blasts
The sheeted towers of sail impend;
While, gathering bale, behind is bred
A livid storm-bow, like a rainbow dead.

At trumpet-call the topmen spring;
And, urged by after-call in stress,
Yet other tribes of tars ascend
The rigging's howling wilderness;
But ere yard-ends alert they win,
Hell rules in heaven with hurricane-fire and din.

.   .   .   .

Plumed with a smoke, a confluent sea,
Heaved in a combing pyramid full,
Spend at its climax, in collapse
Down headlong thundering stuns the hull:
The trophy drops; but, reared again,
Shows Mars' high-altar and contemns the main.

Rebuilt it stands, the brag of arms,
Transferred in site—no thought of where
The sensitive needle keeps its place,
And starts, disturbed, a quiverer there;
The helmsman rubs the clouded glass—
Peers in, but lets trembling portent pass

.　　.　　.　　.　　.　　.　　.　　.　　.

To-night's the night that ends the week—
Ends day and week and month and year:
A fourfold imminent flickering time,
For now the midnight draws anear:
Eight bells! and passing-bells they be—
The Old Year fades, the Old Year dies at sea.

He launched them well. But shall the New
Redeem the pledge the Old Year made,
Or prove a self-asserting heir?
But healthy hearts few qualms invade:
By shot-chests grouped in bays 'tween guns
The gossips chat the grizzled, sea-beat ones.

And boyish dreams some graybeards blab:
"To sea, my lads, we go no more
Who share the Acapulco prize;
We'll all night in, and bang the door;
Our ingots red shall yield us bliss:
Lads, golden years begin to-night with this!"

Released from deck, yet waiting call,
Glazed caps and coats baptized in storm,
A watch of Laced Sleeves round the board
Draw near in heart to keep them warm:
"Sweethearts and wives!" clink, clink, they meet,
And, quaffing, dip in wine their beards of sleet.

"Ay, let the star-light stay withdrawn,
So here her hearth-light memory fling,
So in this wine-light cheer be born,
And honor's fellowship weld our ring—
Honor! our Admiral's aim foretold:
A tomb or a trophy, and lo, 'tis a trophy and gold!"

But he, a unit, sole in rank,
Apart needs keep his lonely state,
The sentry at his guarded door
Mute as by vault the sculptured Fate;
Belted he sits in drowsy light,
And, hatted, nods—the Admiral of the White.

He dozes, aged with watches passed—
Years, years of pacing to and fro;
He dozes, nor attends the stir
In bullioned standards rustling low,
Nor minds the blades whose secret thrill
Perverts overhead the magnet's Polar will.

Less heeds the shadowing three that ply
And follow follow fast in wake,
Untiring wing and lidless eye—
Abreast their course intent they take;
Or sigh or sing, they hold for good
The unvarying flight and fixed inveterate mood.

In dream at last his dozings merge,
In dream he reaps his victory's fruit:
The Flags-o'-the-Blue, the Flags-o'-the-Red,
Dipped flags of his country's fleets salute
His Flag-o'-the-White in harbor proud—
But why should it blench? Why turn to a painted shroud?

The hungry seas they hound the hull,
The sharks they dog the haglets' flight;
With one consent the winds, the waves
In hunt with fins and wings unite,
While drear the harps in cordage sound
Remindful wails for old Armadas drowned.

Ha-yonder! are they Northern Lights?
Or signals flashed to warn or ward?
Yea, signals lanced in breakers high;
But doom on warning follows hard:
While yet they veer in hope to shun,
They strike! and thumps of hull and heart are one.

But beating hearts a drum-beat calls
And prompt the men to quarters go;
Discipline, curbing nature, rules—
Heroic makes who duty know:
They execute the trump's command,
Or in peremptory places wait and stand.

Yet cast about in blind amaze—
As through their watery shroud they peer:
"We tacked from land: then how betrayed?
Have currents swerved us—snared us here?"
None heed the blades that clash in place
Under lamps dashed down that lit the magnet's case.

Ah, what may live, who mighty swim,
Or boat-crew reach that shore forbid,
Or cable span? Most victors drown—
Perish, even as the vanquished did?
Man keeps from man the stifled moan;
They shouldering stand, yet each in heart how lone.

Some heaven invoke; but rings of reefs
Prayer and despair alike deride
In dance of breakers forked or peaked,
Pale maniacs of the maddened tide;
While, strenuous yet some end to earn,
The haglets spin, though now no more astern.

Like shuttles hurrying in the looms
Aloft through rigging frayed they ply—
Cross and recross—weave and inweave,
Then lock the web with clinching cry
Over the seas on seas that clasp
The weltering wreck where gurgling ends the gasp.

Ah, for the Plate-Fleet trophy now,
The victor's voucher, flags and arms;
Never they'll hang in Abbey old
And take Time's dust with holier palms;
Nor less content, in liquid night,
Their captor sleeps—the Admiral of the White.

Imbedded deep with shells
And drifted treasure deep,
Forever he sinks deeper in
Unfathomable sleep—
His cannon round him thrown,
His sailors at his feet,
The wizard sea enchanting them
Where never haglets beat.

On nights when meteors play
And light the breakers' dance,
The Oreads from the caves
With silvery elves advance;
And up from ocean stream,
And down from heaven far,
The rays that blend in dream
The abysm and the star.

SUGGESTED BY THE RUINS
OF A MOUNTAIN-TEMPLE IN ARCADIA,
ONE BUILT BY THE ARCHITECT OF THE PARTHENON

Like stranded ice when freshets die
These shattered marbles tumbled lie:
    They trouble me.

What solace?—Old in inexhaustion,
Interred alive from storms of fortune,
    The quarries be!

PUZZLEMENT
AS TO A FIGURE LEFT SOLITARY ON A UNIQUE
FRAGMENT OF GREEK BASSO-RILIEVO

A crescent brow—a quiver thrown
Behind the shoulder. A huntress, own.
It needs be Artemis. But, nay,
It breathes too much of Eve's sweet way,
And Artemis is high, austere,
Chill as her morn, a goddess mere.

She bends, and with one backward hand
Adjusts her buskin light,
The sidelong face upturned—how arch!
Sure, *somebody* meets her sight.

But never virgin on another
Virgin, or approaching brother
Turned a look like that, I wis.
Profane, if meant for Artemis!
Why, could one but piece out the stone—
Complete restore its primal state,
Some handsome fellow would be shown,
Some Lover she would fascinate
By that arch look.—
                    Nay—can it be?
Again methinks 't is Artemis.
Rogue of a Greek! and is it she?
Show'st thou the goddess, human yet—
The austere Artemis a coquette?
If so in sooth, some latter age
In faith's decay begot thine art—
Such impudence of sweet persiflage!

THE CONTINENTS

From bright Stamboul Death crosses o'er;
Beneath the cypress evermore
His camp he pitches by the shore
    Of Asia old.

Requiting this unsocial mood
Stamboul's inmyrtled multitude
Bless Allah and the sherbert good
    And Europe hold.

Even so the cleaving Bosphorous parts
Life and Death.—Dissembling hearts!
Over the gulf the yearning starts
    To meet—infold!